Fun with Kites

The eighteen kites in this book are simple in concept and based on familiar designs, for building at home. Any one of them can be flown within about an hour of beginning construction, although decoration may take longer.

The actual size of the kites is largely irrelevant. In general, a small kite is harder to fly than a large one. It is the proportions of the kite, and its symmetry, that are important. A lop-sided kite simply won't fly.

Use this book as a guide. Both exact dimensions of the kite shown and the proportions for building a large or small version are given in the instructions.

The kites vary in complexity, and in the materials required. Most of the materials can be found around your home, or bought cheaply at a local shop. Some of the kites can be built in a matter of minutes, while others take a little more time and tax one's ingenuity.

All the kites in the book have been flown to an altitude of around sixty meters; they could fly much higher. In light winds even the largest of the kites can be held by a four-year-old — but such is the enthusiasm for kite-flying that children don't stand much of a chance when adults are standing by to 'help'!

For three thousand years kite-flying has been a hobby for people of all ages. During one flying session, we had four generations of the family taking part. Making and flying kites is a family pursuit, and that's one of the reasons why it's so much fun.

Special thanks to...

*Jemima and Jenny Dyson, the Skipper and
Mrs.'Oskins, and Opa Jaap; Polly, Munro, Marcus,
Petronella and Rosalind Gunn; Danielle and Sally
James; Christopher, Jonathan and Matthew Bigg;
Emma Craven; Edward and Louise Powell; Sara and
Anthony Corless*

...who flew the kites.

GOING METRIC

In this book you will find two systems of measurement. The first
set of figures refers to the customary system and the second to
the metric. Wherever possible both sets of measurements have
been worked out in round numbers, but remember that this
means that the customary and metric figures are *not* equivalent,
so make sure you only work with one set of figures.

John and Kate Dyson

FUN WITH KITES

How to make eighteen beautiful kites

Barron's

First published by Angus & Robertson (U.K.) Ltd. 1976
Copyright © John Dyson 1976

First U.S. Edition — 1978

Barron's Educational Series, Inc.
113 Crossways Park Drive
Woodbury, New York 11797

ISBN: 0-8120-5139-4

Library of Congress Catalog Card Number: 77-071707

Design: Colin Reed
Paintings: Brian Robins
Photographs: John Dyson
Instructional Drawings: Richard Draper

Fabric dyes and dyepaints: Dylon International Ltd.

Printed in Italy

Contents

The story of kites

Kites have always played an important part in people's lives. The Japanese name for a kite (*tako*) means an octopus; the Chinese word (*feng-cheng*) a wind-harp; the Indian (*patang*) a feather and the German word is *drache*, meaning a dragon. This shows just how differently people have felt toward kites over the centuries and in different countries. Kites have not only been used as toys, but for catching food; as religious objects, and quite often as weapons of war.

The first known use of a kite was by a Chinese general in 200 B.C. The general needed to calculate the exact distance of the enemy's fortress walls so that he could build a tunnel underneath them. He did this by flying a kite low over the walls and then measuring the length of the string he had used. A simple idea, but it worked.

Kites originated in China but in fact they have been popular with all eastern and Pacific peoples since long before the birth of Christ. Kites were often a part of daily life (the Samoans used them to pull their canoes, the Koreans used them for catching fish) and in time they took on religious and magical significance.

On the ninth day of the ninth month in the Far East each country celebrated its Kite Day. A kite with the words *Bad luck away, good luck stay* painted on it was cut adrift in order to banish evil spirits. The Maoris launched special birdkites to pacify their war gods and they sang a kite song as the kites rose in the air. The kite was an omen. If it flew smoothly, they would do well in battle; if it fell, they would lose.

Traditional eastern kites were made of rice paper or silk, over bamboo frames. They had faces of birds and animals in bright colors and some of the earliest Chinese and Japanese ones are known to have been as much as 65 feet high, weighing nearly a ton in all. Other kites were smaller and more delicate, and sometimes the bamboo was perforated to make the wind whistle through. These musical kites, or "wind-harps" made a gentle, sad sound and were sometimes flown from rooftops all night to ward off evil spirits.

Until recently kite-fighting was a very popular sport in Southeast Asia. The contestants glued broken glass to their kite-strings so that when one kite overtook another it would cut it down. It was a complicated game with 72 rules and used female kites and male kites. The female kites chased the male kites and looped nooses round them in order to score. In some provinces of Malaya competition became so intense that kite-fighting had to be banned, while in Japan sharp, curved knives were attached to the fighting kites.

A legendary Japanese, named Kakinoki Kinsuke once tried to steal a golden dolphin by kite. The dolphin was fixed high up on the palace of Nagoya and Kinsuke flew over it, pulled by his accomplice, only to find that it was fixed fast. He came away with a few golden fins in his hand and was boiled in oil, with his entire family, for his pains.

In 1752 Benjamin Franklin flew his famous kite in a thunderstorm and discovered "electric fires". (The great inventor had been an imaginative child and as a boy he had used a kite to tow him across a lake as he floated along on his back. He drifted for nearly a mile.)

People were continually inventing new uses for kites and in 1822 an Englishman, George Pocock, designed a light carriage to be pulled by kites. It was called the *char-volant* (flying chariot) and could go

at up to twenty miles per hour. The story goes that when Pocock arrived at a toll-gate the old lady in charge was so confused as to how to describe this peculiar vehicle that she did not know what to charge and let it go through free.

In the 1830s a Franklin Kite Club was formed in America in honor of the inventor and the gentlemen members succeeded in towing a kite-powered sled across the ice. They also sent a kitten up in a basket and landed it safe and sound. These experiments ushered in a century of development of the kite as a means of researching the phenomenon of flight, and for taking high altitude meteorological measurements.

In the 1880s an Australian, Lawrence Hargrave, pioneered the first box kites in Europe. As a specialist in aerodynamics he used the kites to test his theories of flight and it was his work that paved the way for the Wright brothers who, in 1899, made their first step toward the development of the airplane by flying a controlled box kite.

Hargrave was followed by Captain Baden-Powell (brother of the founder of the Scout Movement) who in 1894 built the first really successful man-carrying kite. It was a group of kites tied together and it raised its pilot a hundred feet up in the air.

In wartime kites have been used extensively, for signalling, for carrying lamps, flags, and even for dropping propaganda leaflets. In the last War allied airmen who had been shot down over the sea used kites to lift aerials for sending distress signals and German U-boats lifted up observers in kites flown from their conning towers.

What are kites made of?

In peacetime kites have been used for meteorological purposes. By the end of the last century the US Weather Bureau had more than a score of weather stations sending up high-flying kites daily to take temperature readings and other measurements. This continued until the 1930s when the kites were superseded by balloons; in any case the great number of high kites in the sky was becoming something of a menace to aircraft!

Kites have a long and continuing history and colorful records are still being made. In 1969 a group of schoolchildren in Indiana in the USA launched a train of nineteen small kites. They let out more than ten miles of line and in seven hours their kites reached an altitude of 35,531 feet.

Strong and light materials are what make a successful kite. Traditional oriental kites were made of fine tissue paper pasted on match-thin strips of bamboo which was bent into interesting shapes. Western kites have always tended to be made of stronger stuff, such as lightweight canvas or aluminium foil.

But exciting kites can be made from a wide assortment of materials that you are likely to find around at home — old sheets, remnants of dress materials, newspaper, brown wrapping and Christmas papers and polyethylene bags.

Each of the kites in this book was made from such ordinary household materials. The list of materials required for each kite is intended only as a guide: you should make use of whatever you can find.

THE FRAME

For the long, straight sticks required in the construction of most kites, dowels measuring ¼"/5 mm in diameter are the best. Bamboo is suitable for the upright "backbone" stick of a kite but not for any stick which lies across the kite or which has to be bent, because bamboo is not of an even thickness and the kite will not be symmetrical.

Flexible sticks are more difficult to find. For the kites in this book flexible sticks were made up by joining together with wire, short thin sticks sold in most hardware shops for use in flower-pots. A stick such as a dowel will often bend further if it is first soaked in water for a couple of hours.

The wire used to bind the sticks together, and to join the outer ends of the sticks when required, is thin, soft garden wire; brass wire used for hanging picture frames is also suitable. These wires are easy to work with the fingers, can be tightened with pliers, and can be cut with old scissors.

Strong parcel string is better for kites than nylon because the knots do not loosen so easily. When using string to join sticks together, it helps to smear the binding with modeling glue.

THE COVERING

Lightweight fabric with close weave is suitable for kites. An old sheet is ideal. If you have to buy materials, choose garment-lining fabric which is very cheap and comes in a wide variety of plain colors. It's important that the criss-cross weave of the material is aligned exactly with the vertical and horizontal center-lines of the kite. Otherwise, when the material is stretched, it will distort and the kite will not be symmetrical.

Fabric is easy to work but the edges have to be protected against fraying. It is helpful to use a sewing machine but this is by no means essential. Decorations can be sewn, stapled or glued (with special fabric glue) to the kite.

Newspaper, brown wrapping paper, cellophane, tissue paper or Christmas wrapping papers also make good kite coverings — especially for kites being made by young people. They can be joined together, and attached to the frame, by staples, paper paste, or clear cellophane tape, and decorated with felt pens or poster paint.

One of the quickest materials to use is clear polyethylene. You can buy this in large sheets from hardware shops, or you can find it in the kitchen — by opening out an unused trash can liner. The polyethylene can be clear or colored, and is easily decorated with permanent felt markers. Clear cellophane tape can be used for sticking it down.

DECORATIONS

Kites are made to be seen from far away, so decorations should be big, bold and bright. The most important thing is to choose a suitable color for the covering; if it is to be fabric, the decoration must be thought out carefully when you choose the material. Natural fiber cloths such as cotton or silk can be dyed, and some beautiful designs can be achieved by tie-dying. (See Mr. Sundrop, page 23, for example).

Crêpe paper, Christmas decorations such as tinsel and stars, scraps of brightly colored materials, ribbons and felt markers all come in handy for decoration. Patterns can be painted on, stapled, stuck on with clear cellophane tape, or tacked to the kite with large stitches, using double thread.

If you start with plain material or paper, patterns can be added using thick felt marker pens. In fact, the kite-maker can make use of almost anything for decoration, from milk-bottle tops to household emulsion. But enthusiasm should be tempered by a plane-maker's eye because it is important not to overload the kite, and so impede its flight.

TOOLS FOR KITE-MAKING

Scissors
Pinking shears
Measuring tape
Small wood-saw
Marking pen
Needle and thread
Staple-gun
Sewing machine
Paper-clips and clothes-pins
Hand-drill
Penknife
Pliers

DITTY BAG

When going out to fly kites take these tools and spare parts which will cope with most on-the-spot repair jobs:

Pliers
Length of wire
Scissors
Spare twine
Staple-gun
Small safety-pins
Penknife
Glue

Why a kite needs a tail

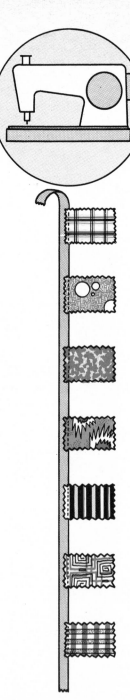

Without a tail a flat-surface kite — like most of the kites in this book — will spin all over the sky and crash into the ground. A tail keeps it upright and well balanced.

The tail can be as simple as long pieces of wide ribbon, or it can be an elaborate chain of colored rosettes made of paper. Both look beautiful, swishing and swaying through the air behind the kite. The important thing is not weight but wind resistance. It is the friction of the wind blowing over the tail that helps it to keep the kite upright.

Kites can fly without tails (such as the Malay Bow Kite on page 79, and the Nagasaki Fighting Kite on page 75). These are kept upright by the flexibility of the fabric from which they are made. The pressure of the wind arches the material against the frame in such a way that the kite is steadied by the aerodynamic effect.

Most people who have trouble flying kites, particularly kites that are bought in shops, make the mistake of trying to use tails that are not nearly long enough. It's better to have a tail that is too long rather than one too short. In a good breeze a hexagonal kite like Mr. Sundrop (page 23) will easily lift a tail 100'/31 m long.

The ideal length of tail is one that, if it were just a little bit shorter, would let the kite dive out of control. This can only be found by trial and error. One rule of thumb is that the tail must be *at least* six times the width of the kite.

Tails can be fixed to the kites with safety pins, paper clips, staples, stitches, or tied to curtain rings sewn to the fabric of the kite. The ribbon-type tails do not tangle easily but other types can quickly get into a dreadful mess: when not in use these should be wrapped round and round a small cardboard box.

Patch tail   Easy to handle and quick to make, this is the tail that is ideal for most of the kites in this book. It is made by machine-sewing (or stapling) rectangular patches of brightly colored material to long lengths of cotton tape which are then knotted together. The patches should be about 6 x 4"/15 x 10 cm, attached to a tape ½"/1 cm wide at intervals of about 4"/10 cm. If the patches are cut from waste scraps of material using pinking shears they will be less prone to fraying.

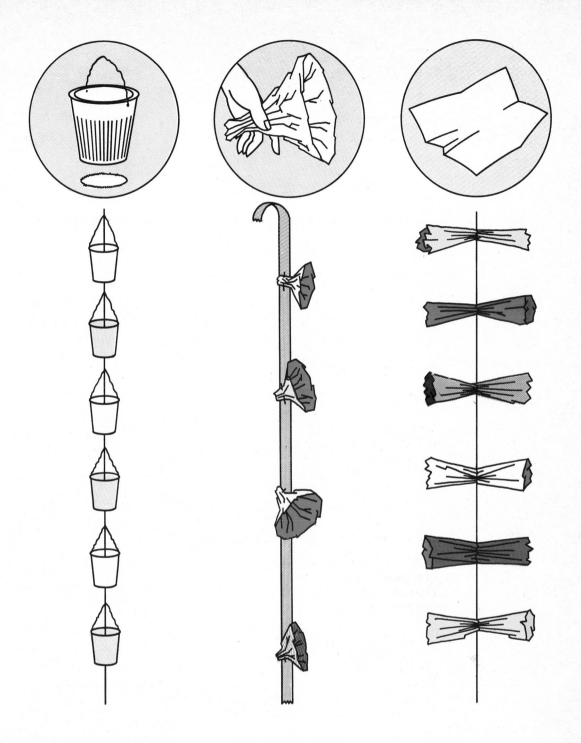

Wind cups This tail is made from paper or plastic cups which are joined together with string. First the bottoms are cut out of the cups so they are like wind funnels, then a string handle is put on each cup, like a bucket handle. Finally, a long string is threaded up through all the cups and the handles are tied to it at intervals of about 8"/20 cm.

Rosette tail Made of brightly colored paper and string, this tail is very decorative but is liable to tangle easily. It is made by cutting out circles of paper about 16"/40 cm in diameter. Each piece of paper is then bunched in the center and the gathers are stapled or tied together and fixed to a long string or piece of cotton tape.

Paper bunches Traditional kite tail in Western countries and probably the quickest and simplest to make, it comprises merely pieces of newspaper, crepe paper or polyethylene and string or tape. The paper is cut into squares of about 8"/20 cm. Each square is gathered in the center and tied to the string or tape at intervals of 4-8"/10-20 cm.

Making a bridle

The bridle is the arrangement of strings or tapes by which the flying line is attached to the kite. If the line is attached in only one place the kite wobbles so much that it loses all lift.

A kite is designed to fly at an angle to the wind. This angle must be precisely set before the kite will fly — by adjusting the bridle.

There are many different types of bridle but for all the kites in this book two simple and very similar bridles have been designed — a two-part bridle and a three-part bridle.

The best material for a bridle is cotton tape about ½"/125 mm wide, but it can also be made of thick string. For a two-part bridle about 6 ft/2 m of string or tape is required; for a three-part bridle, 8ft/3 m.

The special knot made by the center part passing through the brass curtain ring is designed so it can be easily loosened. Adjustment is made by loosening this knot and sliding the ring either forwards or backwards along the tape. The best angle is found mainly by trial and error, and by making small adjustments of less than an inch (2 cm).

In a three-part bridle it is essential that the two upper parts are exactly equal in length or the kite will dive to one side.

Adjustments also have to be made according to the strength of the wind. On calm days the kite will fly best nearer the vertical position; in stronger winds the adjusting ring will have to be moved forward an inch or two to pull the top of the kite nearer to the horizontal position.

Two-part bridle

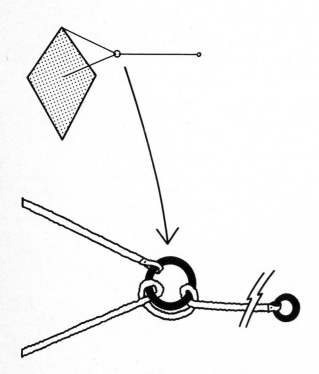

Three-part bridle

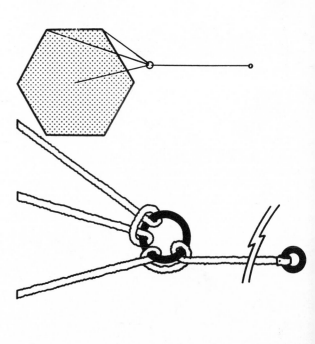

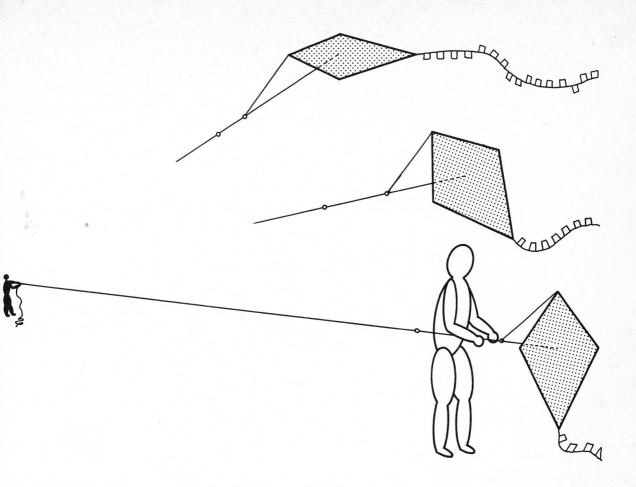

Adjusting the bridle With the line held taut by a helper, walk the kite about 100'/ 30 m down-wind. Adjust the bridle so the kite is held in a vertical attitude. Let the wind fill the kite so it is nearly flying — it may need a steadying hand to stop it waving from side to side. Then loosen the center knot and move the brass curtain ring about 1"/ 250 mm forward. Let the kite fly again: now leaning forward into the wind, it should begin to climb. If it does not climb high enough bring the kite down again and move the ring a little further forward still. The ring is too far forward if the kite nose-dives beyond the horizontal.

How to tie the special knot

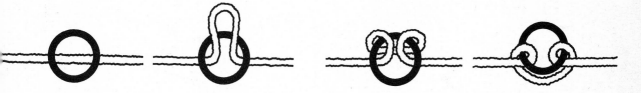

1. Lay the ring on the string or tape of the bridle.
2. Draw a loop through the center of the ring

3. Fold the loop over the back of the ring
4. Continue folding the loop over until it is under the ring; pull tight.

Reel and line for kites

A strong and easy-to-hold reel is essential for kite-flying because the pull of the kite is considerable. Without a reel the line will burn your fingers severely as it runs out, will cut into your hands when the kite is flying, and will tangle easily.

Two reels that are easy and cheap to make at home are pictured here.

Kite-flying line should be thin, light and strong. In China hundreds of years ago colored silks were used, but today's nylon products are equally good, and easier to come by! Braided fishing line is ideal, but expensive — it's better to hunt around your local hardware shops to see what you can find. The line should have a breaking strain of at least 40 lbs/20 kgs. A length of 100 yards/100 m is sufficient.

Make sure that the end of the line is tied firmly to the reel so the kite won't escape. A round turn and two half-hitches is a simple knot for attaching the line to the bridle. Never fly a kite when the line is wet, and never use a wire line — you might get an electric shock from lightning in the clouds.

When flying a kite always make use of the reel — don't be tempted to take the string off the reel and let it run through your bare hands. Your fingers are likely to be burned or cut, and when you let go of the line at the sudden pain the kite could be damaged.

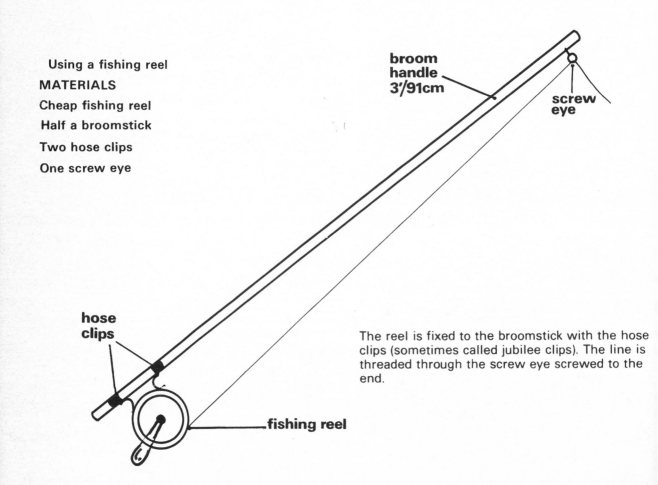

Using a fishing reel

MATERIALS

Cheap fishing reel

Half a broomstick

Two hose clips

One screw eye

broom handle 3'/91cm

screw eye

hose clips

fishing reel

The reel is fixed to the broomstick with the hose clips (sometimes called jubilee clips). The line is threaded through the screw eye screwed to the end.

How to fly a kite

Making a cradle reel

MATERIALS

Two dowels, length about 10"/25 cm

Two flat pieces of boxwood, approx 1½"/4 cm wide, ½"/1 cm thick, 15"/38 cm long

Wood-glue

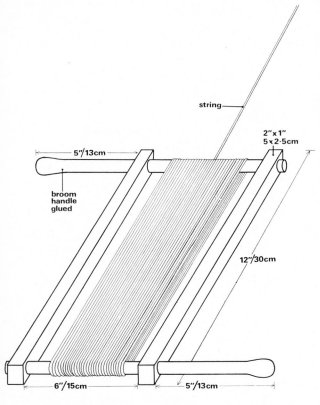

string

2"x1"
5 x 2·5cm

5"/13cm

broom handle glued

12"/30cm

6"/15cm   5"/13cm

This reel is very simple to make and comfortable to hold; it makes lighter work of reeling in the kite than the fishing reel but is more cumbersome to use when launching.

The best kite-flying wind is a steady breeze that's just sufficient to ruffle your hair and stir the leaves on the trees. Gusty winds that bend whole trees and send clouds scudding prompt people to remark "Good weather for kites" but in fact these conditions are too strong. Even on a balmy day when there's scarcely enough breeze to be felt on your cheek it's often possible to fly a lightweight kite which finds its own little breeze as is rises over treetop height.

Only in very calm conditions, when you expect a kite to find a wind once it gets up a bit, should it be necessary to run with a kite. Normally the kite will float from your hand and if it is well balanced and properly stabilized you should be able to fly it while reclining in a deck-chair.

Open areas such as fields, hilltops and beaches are ideal for flying kites. Avoid overhead wires, buildings, roads and trees. Look for a "clean" wind coming over a long stretch of open ground where there are no buildings or trees to make it whirl and eddy in a way that makes kite-flying difficult.

Weather lore : it is highly dangerous to fly a kite in bad weather : your line will get wet and act as a conductor for any static charge of electricity building up in the clouds.

How to fly a kite

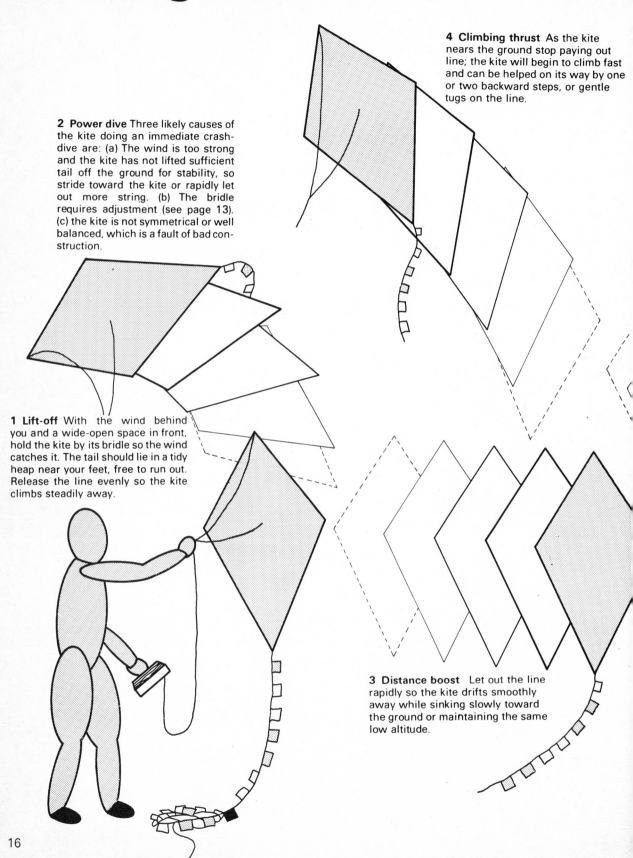

4 Climbing thrust As the kite nears the ground stop paying out line; the kite will begin to climb fast and can be helped on its way by one or two backward steps, or gentle tugs on the line.

2 Power dive Three likely causes of the kite doing an immediate crash-dive are: (a) The wind is too strong and the kite has not lifted sufficient tail off the ground for stability, so stride toward the kite or rapidly let out more string. (b) The bridle requires adjustment (see page 13). (c) the kite is not symmetrical or well balanced, which is a fault of bad construction.

1 Lift-off With the wind behind you and a wide-open space in front, hold the kite by its bridle so the wind catches it. The tail should lie in a tidy heap near your feet, free to run out. Release the line evenly so the kite climbs steadily away.

3 Distance boost Let out the line rapidly so the kite drifts smoothly away while sinking slowly toward the ground or maintaining the same low altitude.

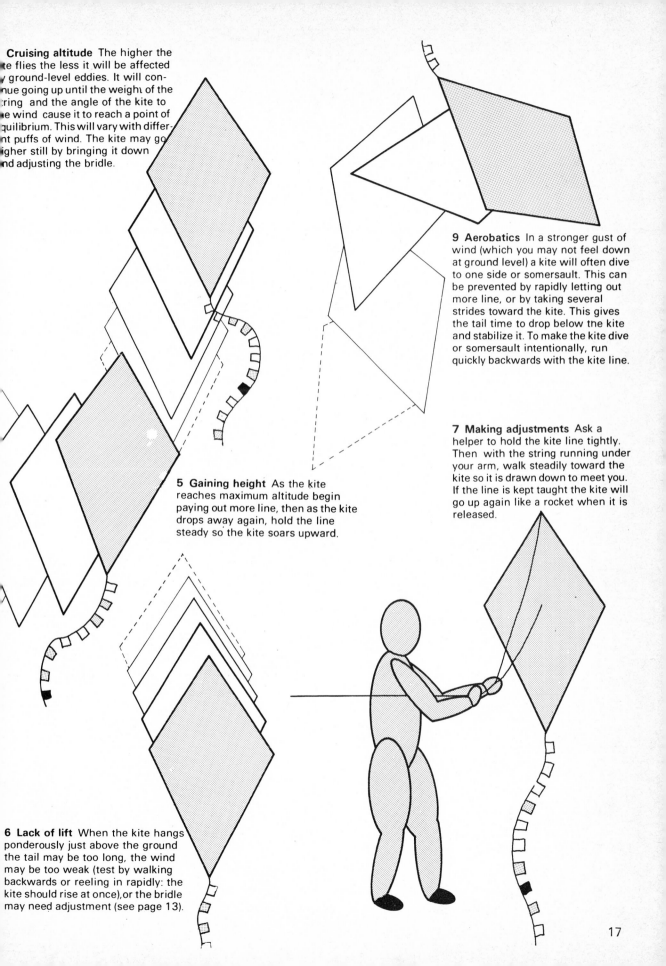

Cruising altitude The higher the kite flies the less it will be affected by ground-level eddies. It will continue going up until the weight of the string and the angle of the kite to the wind cause it to reach a point of equilibrium. This will vary with different puffs of wind. The kite may go higher still by bringing it down and adjusting the bridle.

9 Aerobatics In a stronger gust of wind (which you may not feel down at ground level) a kite will often dive to one side or somersault. This can be prevented by rapidly letting out more line, or by taking several strides toward the kite. This gives the tail time to drop below the kite and stabilize it. To make the kite dive or somersault intentionally, run quickly backwards with the kite line.

7 Making adjustments Ask a helper to hold the kite line tightly. Then with the string running under your arm, walk steadily toward the kite so it is drawn down to meet you. If the line is kept taught the kite will go up again like a rocket when it is released.

5 Gaining height As the kite reaches maximum altitude begin paying out more line, then as the kite drops away again, hold the line steady so the kite soars upward.

6 Lack of lift When the kite hangs ponderously just above the ground the tail may be too long, the wind may be too weak (test by walking backwards or reeling in rapidly: the kite should rise at once),or the bridle may need adjustment (see page 13).

FLOATING FACES

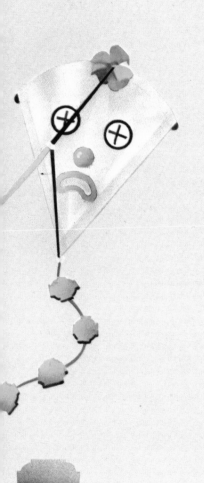

Happy and sad clowns

Happy and sad clowns

Good fliers and easy to make, one of these clown kites can be made in about fifteen minutes. In the sky they weave and flutter like clowns tumbling and skylarking in the circus ring. Being light, they are ideal for small children to make and fly. But they also tend to be easily affected by wind eddies close to the ground so the higher they fly the steadier they become. In strong breezes they require surprisingly long tails. Instead of a covering of polyethylene, practically any household material, such as brown paper or strong cellophane, may be used.

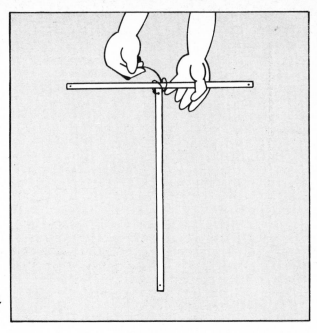

Stage 1 Drill a hole at each end of both sticks. Balance the more flexible stick on top of the other to form a T. Thread wire or string through the top hole of the upright and bind the vertical stick firmly to the mid-point of the horizontal. Add a loop for attaching the bridle later.

MATERIALS

2 light sticks of equal length (one must be able to bend a little) 30"/76 cm long
1 sheet of polyethylene (an opened-out trash can liner is ideal) about 30"/76 cm square
Strong twine or thin garden wire
Cellophane tape
Colored paper for tail and decoration

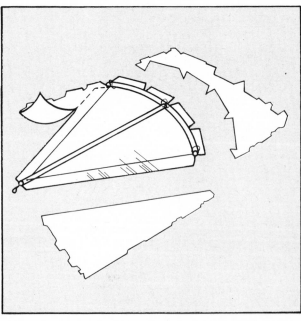

Stage 4 Lay the frame on a sheet of polyethylene or an opened-out plastic trash-can liner. Cut around the frame, leaving a one inch/25 mm margin. Make V-shaped cuts where necessary so that the material will fold over the arched top of the frame.

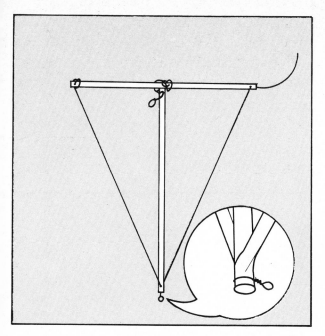

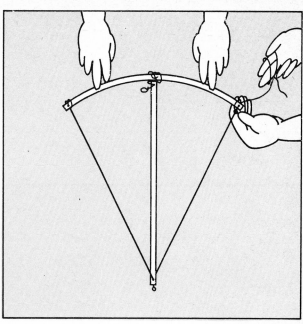

Stage 2 Fix a long piece of thin, strong twine or thin garden wire to one end of the cross-piece. Thread it through the hole in the bottom of the vertical stick. Bring it up to the hole at the opposite end of the cross-piece and thread it ready for tying.

Stage 3 Steadily press the ends of the cross-piece downwards, taking up the slack on the string and keeping the arch equal on each side. The bend does not have to be very great: if the vertical is 30"/76 cm, the ends of the cross-piece should be bent down about 6"/15cm. Tie the string or wire firmly.

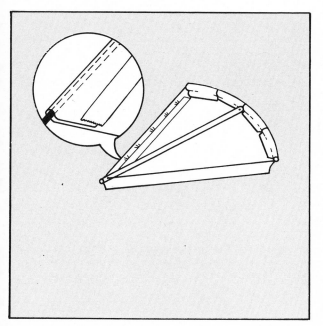

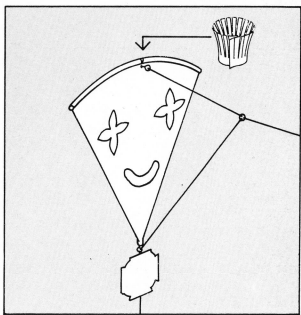

Stage 5 Fold the edges over the frame, pulling the polyethylene taut, and stick it down firmly with cellophane tape. Use thin wire, such as a straightened paper-clip, to make a small loop at the bottom of the frame for attaching the tail and a two-part bridle (see page 12). Make a small hole and bring the top loop through to the front.

Stage 6 Decorate the kite with a clown's face, using felt pens. The colors show up better from afar if outlined with a thick black line. Crêpe paper can be cut to form a top-knot. The tail (page 11) can be made of matching paper on white tape. Attach bridle to top and bottom loops.

Mr. Sundrop

A cheerful flier, it pulls briskly in any wind yet soars steadily if the tail is long enough. It has the simple hexagon shape which forms the basis of several other kites in this book and can be made in less than an hour. For easy carrying it collapses within seconds into a shape like a rolled umbrella. Size can vary from 12"/30 cm to 6'/2 m but in strong winds a large kite this shape pulls very hard. The tail should be at least six times the width of the kite, but can be much longer.

MATERIALS

Large piece of material such as an old sheet about
44"/112 cm square
3 straight sticks each about 42"/107 cm long
1 curtain ring or short piece of flexible wire
Length of cotton tape or string

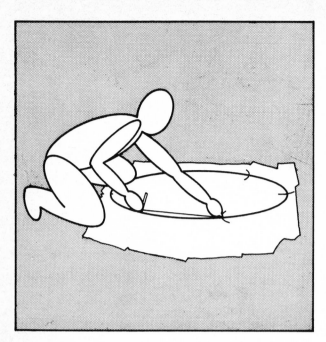

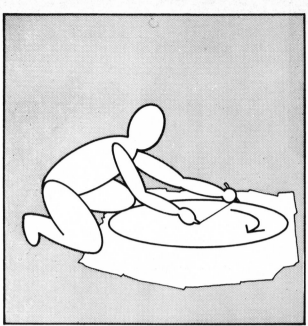

Stage 1 Lay the material out flat and find its approximate centre. Make a drawing compass with a marker pencil held in a loop at the end of a piece of string and inscribe a circle as shown. The radius of the circle of the kite pictured is 21"/53 cm.

Stage 2 Using exactly the same length of string, start from any position on the circumference of the circle and lightly inscribe an arc. Move the string to the point where the arc intersects the circumference and inscribe another arc. Repeat so that the circle is marked at six equally spaced points.

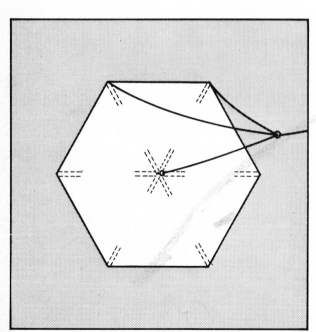

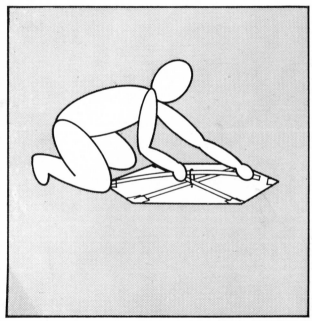

Stage 5 Cut the sticks equally so they are about 1"/25 mm longer than the diagonal measurement of the hexagon. Thread them through the curtain ring or a small loop of wire; insert the ends in opposite pockets. The material should be gently taut; if necessary shorten the sticks a little.

Stage 6 The intersection of the sticks and the curtain ring or wire should lie over the centre of the hexagon. Make a small hole in the fabric below it. Attach a three-part bridle (see page 12) to the ring and two adjacent corner points (which now become the top of the kite).

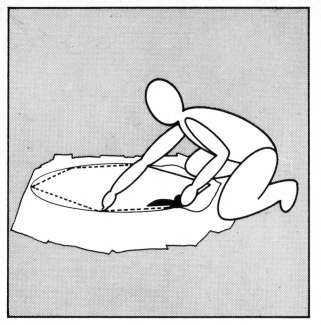

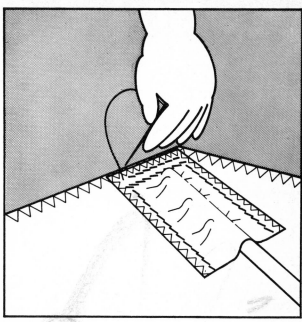

Stage 3 To complete the hexagonal shape, join up each mark. Now cut around the hexagon. To prevent fraying either cut with pinking shears, machine-sew all round using zig-zag stitch, or leave a margin of about ½" / 12 mm and turn up a narrow hem all the way round.

Stage 4 From the discarded corners cut small rectangles of fabric to make the six pockets, each one just wide enough to take the sticks and 2-3"/5-8 cm long. Reinforce the bottom of each pocket with a double seam to prevent the sticks from chafing holes in the fabric.

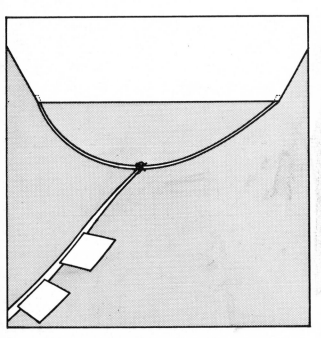

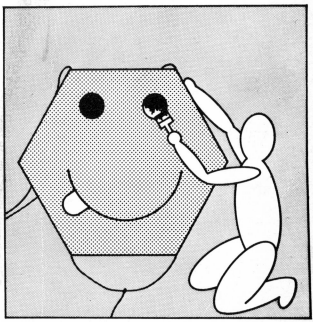

Stage 7 To the bottom points of the kite sew a length of cord which should hang below the kite in a shallow loop. At the mid-point of the cord sew on a curtain ring for the tail (see page 11).

Stage 8 If the sticks are removed the material can then be tie-dyed (like Mr. Sundrop) and the eyes and mouth marked with dye-paint or felt-tipped marker pens. Alternatively the kite can be made from patterned material, or colored scraps can be tacked or glued on.

Black-eyed Suzy

Black-eyed Suzy

In a steady breeze the pig-tailed girl floats prettily in the sky, her plaits waving as if she were gently nodding her head and smiling. This is one of the simplest and most quickly constructed of all the kites which are made of fabric. It collapses for ease of carrying and is assembled in less than half a minute. The shape of this kite is traditional and in steady winds will often fly with no tail of any kind. The pull is mild and the kite will reach high altitudes.

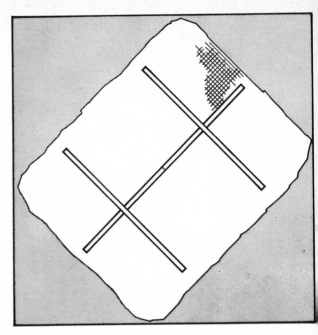

Stage 1 Mark the longer stick into quarters; mark each one with a pencil. Cut the other two sticks to three-quarters its length. Spread out the fabric and position the sticks over it as shown: they should align exactly with the criss-cross weave of the fabric.

MATERIALS

3 light, straight, strong sticks, two 36"/91 cm, one 48"/122 cm long
1 rectangle of plain, colored fabric about 40" x 52"/102 x 132 cm
Small piece of flexible wire
Black crêpe paper
Decorative paper
2 curtain rings (see page 12)
Tails 6'/183 cm long

Stage 4 Insert the sticks in the pockets, bending them a little if necessary: when the kite is face down the upright should be below the horizontal sticks. The fabric should be taut enough to eliminate wrinkles. The face and hair can be painted using dyes or acrylic paint.

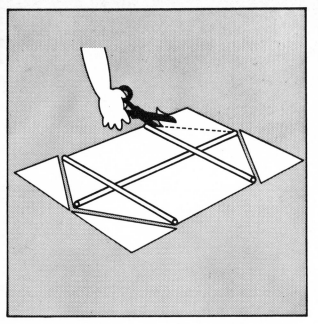

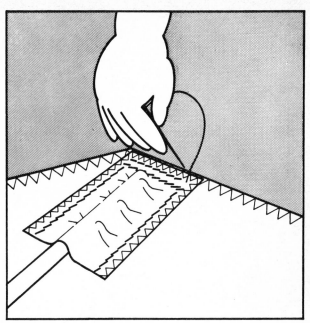

Stage 2 Trim the material to the length and width of the rectangle formed by the sticks, then cut away the corners as shown. When cutting, use pinking shears to prevent fraying of the fabric later. Alternatively, hem the edges or seam them by sewing-machine, using zig-zag stitch.

Stage 3 From the discarded corners cut small rectangles of fabric to make the six pockets, each one just wide enough to take the sticks and 2-3"/5-8 cm long. Reinforce the bottom of each pocket with a double seam to prevent the sticks from chafing holes in the fabric.

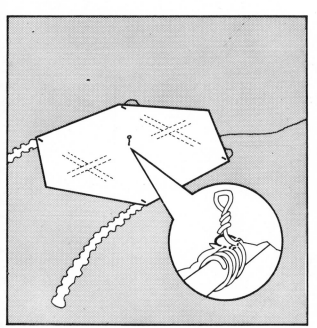

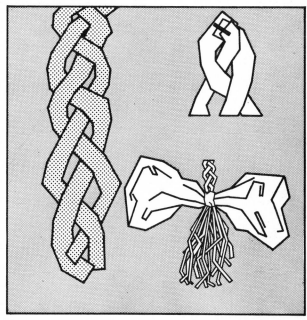

Stage 5 Use the short piece of wire to make a loop for attaching the three-part bridle (see page 12) to the mid-point of the upright stick; a small hole will have to be made in the fabric. Sew or staple the upper bridle tapes to the top corners of the kite; match the color of the tapes to the hair color.

Stage 6 Plait three narrow strips of black crêpe paper for each tail, which is stapled or safety-pinned to the kite. Each tail must be exactly equal in weight: trim one if the kite is lopsided in flight. Pretty bows for the plaits can be made with bunches of shiny Christmas paper.

The War-lord

The War-lord

The trailing moustaches of this fierce oriental War-lord act as a tail to steady the kite. With his squinting eyes and fluttering eyebrows he flies strongly even in a gentle breeze. Like one of the Seven Samurai, he surveys his land from on high with a supercilious air. His square head looks impressive in the sky. The whole kite collapses and rolls up into a slender bundle and is reassembled in a matter of seconds. Colored scraps of material or brightly colored paper, tacked on with needle and thread, form his eyes, mouth and eyebrows.

Stage 1 (This kite can be any size from 1'/30 cm to 5'/150 cm square, depending on the size of your fabric). Lay the fabric flat and check that it is square by measuring. Prevent fraying of the raw edges by hemming, sewing with zig-zag stitch by machine, or trimming with pinking shears.

MATERIALS

1 square of finely woven, lightweight fabric, 36"/91 cm square
3 strong, light, straight sticks 48"/122 cm long
1 brass curtain ring big enough for two sticks to pass through
Scraps of colored material and paper
8 strips of material 1½"/4 cm wide and 1'-12'/30 cm-4 m long, for the tails

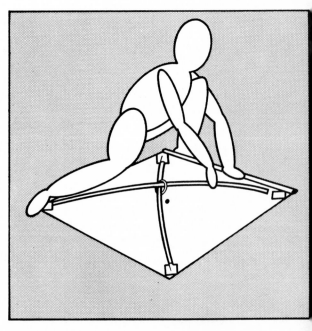

Stage 4 Insert the sticks into the pockets, bending them slightly if necessary, after threading each of them through a brass curtain ring in the center of the kite. Cut a small hole in the fabric beneath the curtain ring. When the sticks are in place the fabric must be taut.

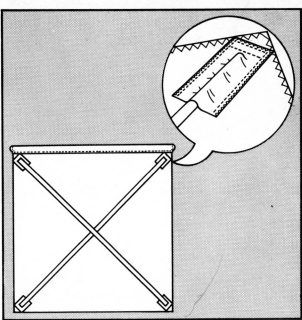

Stage 2 Cut one stick to fit the width of the square. Lay it along the top edge, then fold the fabric over so the stick is enclosed in a narrow hem and sew it in. Stitch up both ends firmly so the fabric is tight along the length of the stick.

Stage 3 Lay the kite face down and cut the two remaining sticks to fit the diagonals of the square. From scrap material cut four rectangular pockets, each just wide enough to take a stick and 2-3"/5-8 cm long. Sew a pocket in each corner, reinforcing the bottom of each with a double seam.

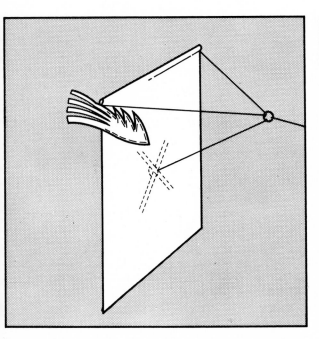

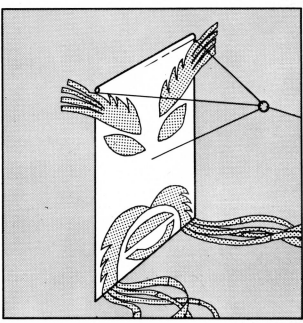

Stage 5 Sew the upper tapes of a three-part bridle (see page 12) to the top corners of the kite. Tie the lower cord to the center ring. Cut the eyebrows to fit and sew them on with large tacking stitches using needle and thread; cut the ends into tassels so they flutter.

Stage 6 Cut scrap material into strips about 1½"/4 cm wide and staple them together to make long trailing whiskers for the tails. Eyes and mouth can be made of paper or material and trimmed to give the War-lord a benign or a fierce expression. In stronger winds longer tails can be added temporarily with safety-pins.

Leaf kite

A GARDEN IN THE SKY

Leaf kite

The most traditional of the many different kite shapes, this flat diamond kite can be made from practically any materials that happen to be on hand, such as thin garden stakes, twine and newspaper. Brown wrapping paper or polyethylene are ideal covering materials but fabrics, tinfoil or cellophane may also be used. Construction takes only a few minutes and the kite will fly in practically any conditions; a tail — long in breezy weather — is always needed. The kite darts about in the sky and is particularly easy for youngsters to make and fly.

Stage 1 (This type of kite can be any size — as tall as 6'/2 m, as small as 1'/30 cm. Cut one stick to about three-quarters the length of the other).
Position the short stick horizontally across the other to form a cross. Ensure that both sides of the cross are equal in width.

MATERIALS

2 straight, strong sticks 36"/91 cm and 48"/122 cm long

1 sheet of strong, thin paper such as brown wrapping paper or Christmas parcel paper about 48"/122 cm square

String or thin garden wire

Cellophane tape or glue

Poster paints for decoration

Tail 40'/12 m long

Stage 4 The frame and its border must be taut, but do not distort the sticks. Lay it face down on the covering material. Cut around it leaving a 1"/2-3 cm margin. Fold the edges over the string or wire and stick them down with cellophane tape or glue so the covering material is taut.

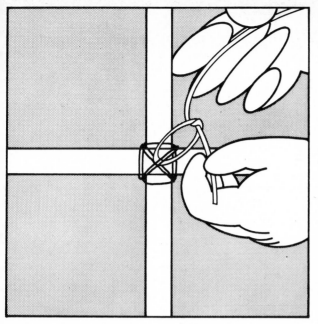

Stage 2 With string or wire securely bind the two sticks together so they are at right angles to each other. To ensure a firm joint, cover the binding with a thin coat of modelling glue. Tie the ends of the string or wire into a small loop for attaching the bridle later.

Stage 3 Drill holes at the ends of each stick. Fix a long piece of string or thin wire to the top stick, then thread it through each hole, and tie it firmly at the top, leaving a second small loop for the bridle.

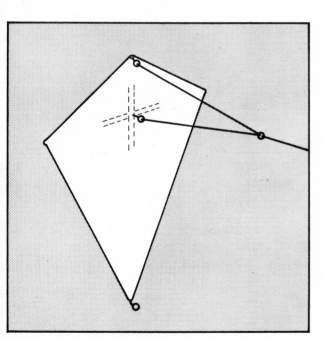

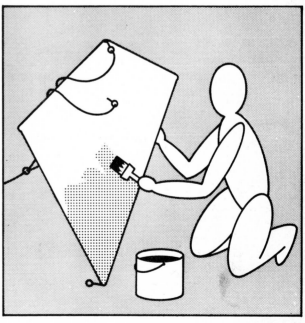

Stage 5 Cut a small hole in the covering material so the loop in the center of the kite will come through; attach the lower tape of a two-part bridle (see page 12). Fix the upper part of the bridle to the loop at the top of the kite. Add another loop to the bottom for attaching the tail.

Stage 6 Poster paints are ideal for decoration if the kite is covered in newspaper or brown paper. Cut-out patterns, spangles, tassels and other decorations can be added with glue or staples. Long streamers can be added on either side. For a leaf design, bright green paint is effective.

Sunflower

Sunflower

Like the magic beanstalk that Jack climbed, the flying flower soars into the sky growing higher and higher, trailing its bright green stem. This round kite is based on the hexagonal shape of Mr. Sundrop (page 23). It is started in exactly the same way but the edges of the circle are not trimmed off. This one is made of an old sheet dyed yellow, then marked with black felt pen. A variety of flower shapes, such as the poppy on page 39, can be made using different colors and decorations. It flies strongly but needs a long tail.

Stage 1 Using string and marking pencil as a drawing compass, inscribe a circle radius 24"/61 cm on the material. (Your kite can be any size from 2'-6'/61-183 cm.) Then, using exactly the same length of string (equal to the radius of the circle) mark six equally spaced points around its circumference.

MATERIALS

Large piece of light material such as an old sheet about 50"/127 cm square

3 straight sticks 50"/127 cm long

1 large curtain ring

12 short, lightweight, flower-pot sticks 17"/43 cm long

Carpet tape (for use on fabric)

Cord or string

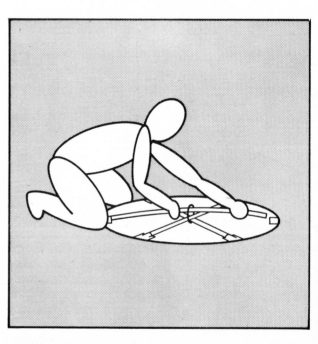

Stage 4 Cut the sticks equally so they are about 1"/25 mm longer than the diameter of the circle. Thread them through the curtain ring; insert the ends in opposite pockets. The material should be gently taut; if necessary shorten the sticks a little.

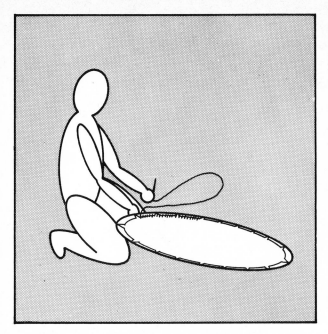

Stage 2 Cut around the circle. To prevent fraying either cut with pinking shears, machine-sew all round using zig-zag stitch, or leave a margin of about ½"/12 mm and turn up a narrow hem all the way round (small V-cuts will be required at intervals to keep the shape of the circle).

Stage 3 From the discarded material cut small rectangles to make the six pockets, each one just wide enough to take the sticks and 2-3"/5-8 cm long. Reinforce the bottom of each pocket with a double seam to prevent the sticks chafing holes in the fabric.

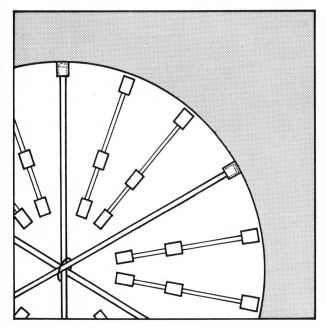

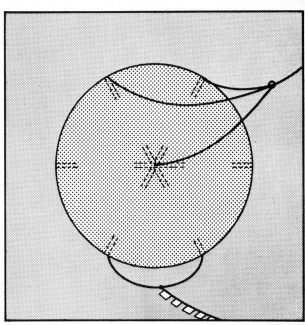

Stage 5 To prevent the edges of the circle between the pockets from folding backwards in the wind it is necessary to support them. Lay two thin flower-pot sticks about 17"/43 cm long in each segment of the circle, as shown, and stick each down firmly with three squares of carpet tape.

Stage 6 The brass ring where the sticks cross should lie over the center of the circle. Make a small hole in the fabric beneath. Attach a three-point bridle (see page 12) to the ring and two top pockets. Stitch a shallow loop of cord to the bottom for attaching the tail (see page 10).

Caterpillar

Caterpillar

No garden is complete without its creepy-crawlies and here is one — a huge, belly-dancing caterpillar. It flies strongly, body swaying and twitching seductively in the breeze. This kite is a certain crowd-stopper in any park. Despite its size (3-5'/91-152 cm) it folds quickly into a narrow bundle for easy carrying. Scope for imaginative decoration is endless: this pink and green chap is happily demure, but fierce hairy black and yellow caterpillars, or militant dragon-like orange and purple ones look impressive as they wriggle up towards the clouds.

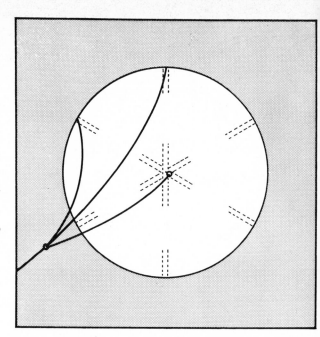

Stage 1 Make the face of the caterpillar in exactly the same way as the sunflower (described on page 40), complete with three straight sticks in six pockets, three-part bridle, and hemmed or sewn edges. But do not bother to reinforce the back of the kite with flower-pot sticks.

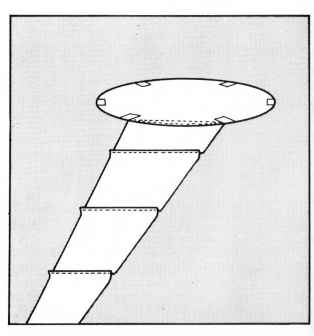

MATERIALS

Large area of colored lightweight material (such as garment-lining fabric) about 50"/127 cm square

3 straight sticks about 50"/127 cm long

8 short sticks 17"/43 cm long

1 large curtain ring

Carpet tape

Colored paper or scraps of material

Length of tail about 8'/244 cm plus streamers; width at top about 20"/51 cm at bottom 6"/15 cm; eyes 10"/25 cm wide.

Stage 4 Join the segments together — by sewing-machine is quickest. Remove the sticks from the face and sew the top of the tail firmly to the hem. Long remnants of material from the tail make colorful streamers which can be attached with a couple of stitches, or stapled.

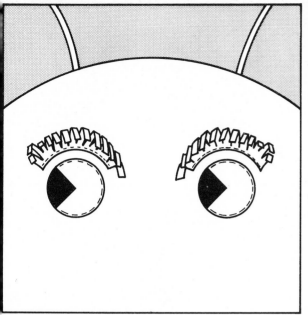

Stage 2 The caterpillar's face is made of colored paper or scraps of material stitched or glued on the fabric; they may look bolder if also outlined in black felt pen. Fringes of crêpe paper make bushy eyebrows. Features such as antennae can be added by attaching wire or thin sticks to the frame.

Stage 3 The tail is about 8'/244 cm long, twice the diameter of the face. Width at the top of the tail should fill the space between the two bottom pockets and the tail should taper to practically nothing. If different-colored segments are used, lay them out in order and trim the edges to shape.

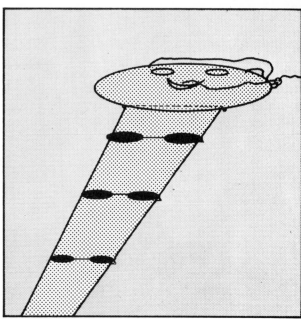

Stage 5 On the back of the tail fasten thin sticks, cut to length, at intervals which correspond to the seams joining the segments; squares of carpet tape stuck over the ends of the sticks will hold them firmly. If more weight must be added later attach more sticks.

Stage 6 Cut out round patches of black material or crêpe paper and stitch, staple or glue them to the front of the tail in pairs, largest at the top and smallest at the bottom. They should correspond with the joints of the segments to look like the caterpillar's feet.

Peacock

One of the most elegant and delicate of kites, the peacock, has two especially beautiful points of flight. With bright sun shining on it the gold medallions of its fanned tail glitter and twinkle as it sways in the breeze. With the soft sun of an evening sky behind it, the full beauty of its semi-transparent fronded tail feathers and the proud swell of its breast are perfectly outlined. For stability, a tail can be attached to the center stick or, if the flexible stick is strong enough, tails can be fixed to the wing-tips.

MATERIALS

1 straight stick 36"/91 cm long
1 flexible stick of even thickness 72"/182 cm long
Thin polyethylene sheet such as a trash can liner about 46"/112 cm square
String and thin wire
Cellophane tape
Colored cellophane and tinsel

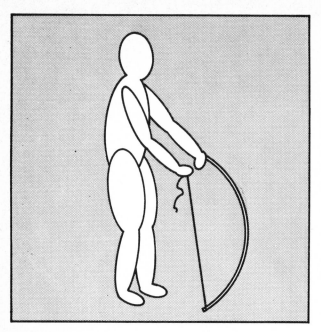

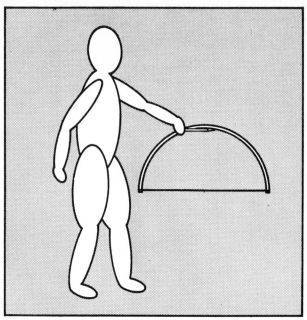

Stage 1 Bore a small hole in the ends of both sticks. Take the long stick and tie a piece of string or thin wire to one end. Carefully bend the stick until it makes nearly a half-circle; it should be able to bend a little further still without snapping.

Stage 2 If necessary soak the stick in water for two hours to increase flexibility. Tie the string or wire to the other end as if stringing a bow. Find the point of balance by hanging the bow on a pencil, then mark.

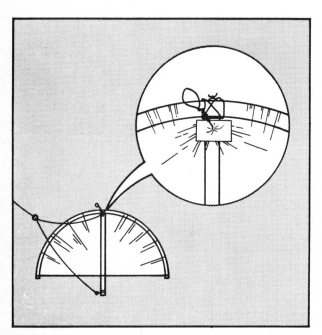

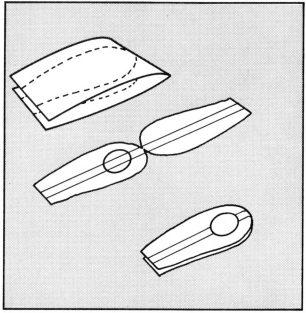

Stage 5 Use short lengths of wire to make loops at the top and bottom of the straight stick. Reinforce the polyethylene with a square of cellophane tape where the wire passes through it. Attach a two-part bridle (see page 12) to the loops. The lower loop will also take the tail.

Stage 6 The kite can now be test-flown if necessary. For decoration, cut doubled-over sheets of cellophane into tear-drop shapes. Reinforce front and back of each with cellophane tape. Choose peacock colors (blue, green, turquoise) carefully. Include some round shapes of gold or silver tinfoil.

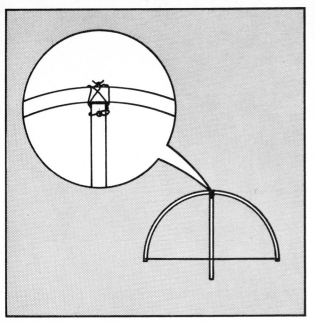

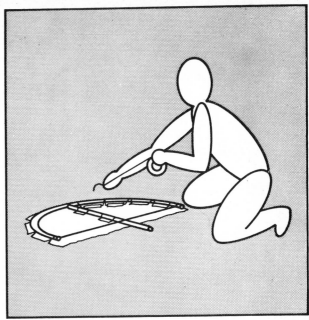

Stage 3 Firmly fix a short length of string or wire to one end of the shorter stick, then tie it to the center mark of the bow. Do not cut or drill the bent stick as this may weaken it. Spread the polyethylene flat and position the frame over it.

Stage 4 Cut around the bent stick and the string, leaving a margin of 2"/5 cm. Make wide V-cuts every 4-6"/10-15 cm. Fold the edges over the bent stick; fasten with cellophane tape. Put cellophane tape over the straight stick but do not fasten the string to the polyethylene covering.

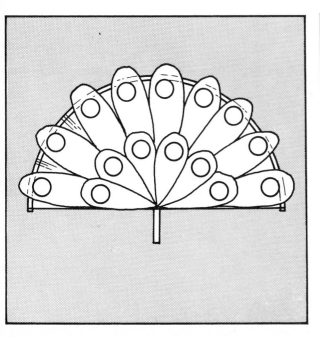

Stage 7 With needle and thread, lightly tack the cut-out shapes to the polyethylene, always stitching through the reinforcing cellophane tape and not through the cellophane. Alternatively, colored paper can be stuck on with glue, or the tail pattern can be drawn directly on to the polyethylene with permanent felt markers.

Stage 8 Cut the body from a piece of colored paper which does not let the light through. This will make a clear silhouette against the sky. It can be stuck down with glue or cellophane tape; if you wish, crown it with a short piece of Christmas tinsel.

FLYING FISH

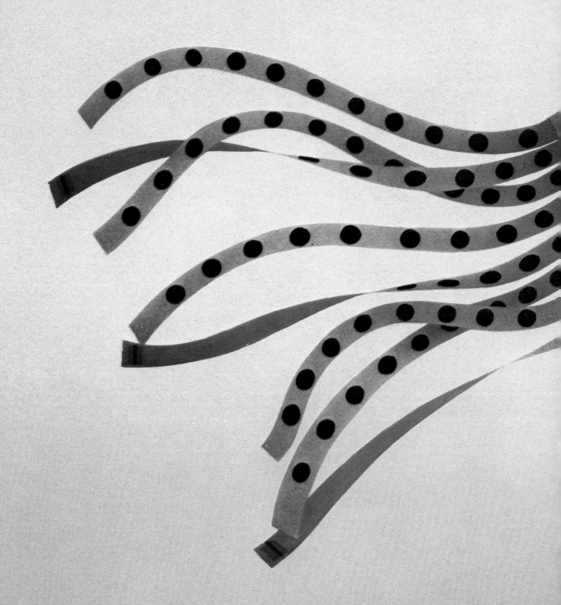

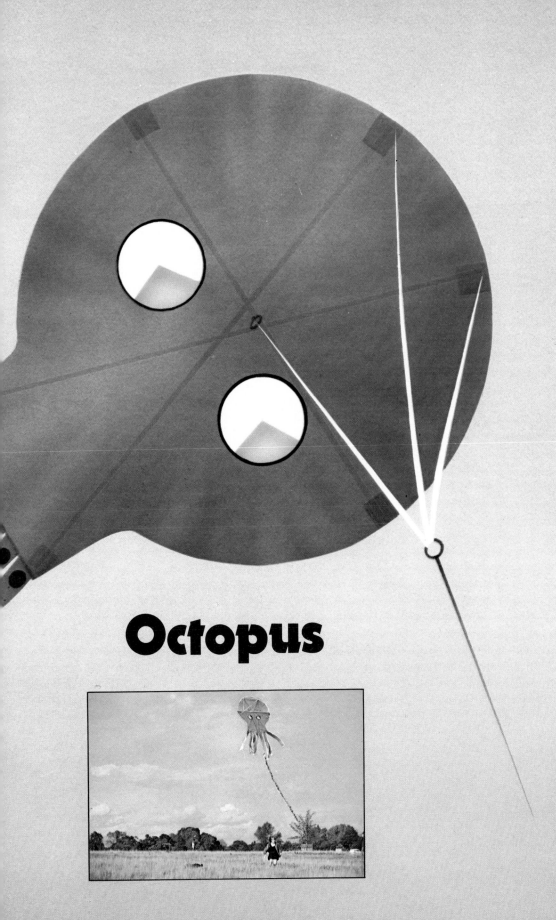

Octopus

Octopus

Here is one menace of which flying fish and hovering angels should beware - a high-flying octopus. When he scoots among the clouds with tentacles quivering the passers-by certainly stop and stare. This kite is a variation of the hexagonal shape. It has a rounded top and a row of eight streamers for legs. In stronger winds it may need a tail as well, which can be attached to one of the center legs or to the back of the kite. If made of dark blue materials the tail will look as if the octopus is taking refuge behind a jet of ink.

Stage 1 (The kite can be from 2-6'/60-200 cm wide.) Using string and marking pencil as a drawing compass, inscribe a circle radius 18"/45 cm, at one end of the material. Mark six equally spaced points around the circumference (see page 24). Between the two lower points mark an apron 4-6"/10-15 cm deep as shown.

MATERIALS

Large piece of light-colored material (2 yards /2 meters of garment-lining material is ideal)
3 straight sticks 42"/107 cm long
5 short lightweight flower-pot sticks about 12"/30 cm long
Colored scraps for decoration
1 brass curtain ring
Carpet tape

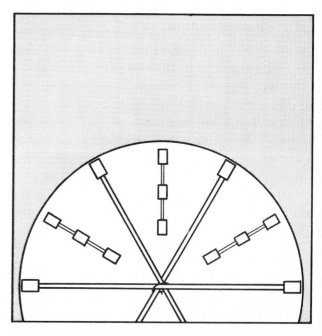

Stage 4 To support the rounded shape of the octopus's head use a light flower-pot stick fixed down firmly with squares of carpet tape midway between each of the four upper pockets. Make a small hole in the fabric beneath the curtain ring and attach a three-point bridle (see page 12).

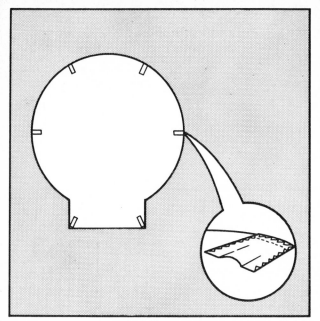

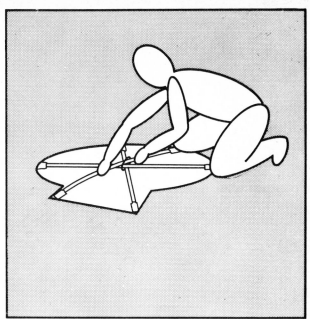

Stage 2 Cut out the kite circle and machine-sew all round the curved edge using zig-zag stitch, or turn up a narrow hem. From discarded material (see page 28) make six rectangular pockets and sew them on, open ends towards the center of the kite, at the bottom corners of the apron and at each of the other four marked points.

Stage 3 Cut the sticks to about 1"/3 cm longer than the measured distance between opposite pockets. Thread them through the curtain ring. Insert the ends in the pockets: the material should be gently taut but if too tight shorten the sticks a little.

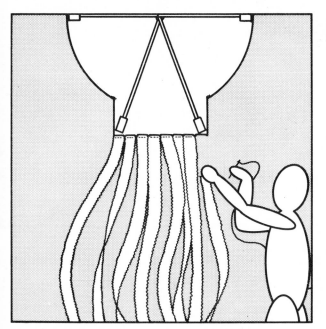

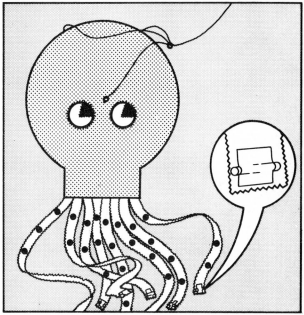

Stage 5 The eight legs, as long as the height of the head of the octopus, can be cut from the same piece of material or made from different colors and stitched to the bottom of the apron. Each leg should be 2-4"/5-10 cm wide and trimmed with pinking shears to prevent fraying.

Stage 6 Cut eight short pieces of stick and fasten them horizontally with carpet tape across the ends of the legs. Patches of colored materials can be sewn on to represent suckers. Eyes and eyebrows and other decorations can be stitched or glued to the head.

Sunfish

Sunfish

The sunfish is a creature of the doldrums. A large and delicate kite, it is built for balmy breezes. Made of very light, bright-yellow seersucker cotton whose pattern gives it a scaly effect so no body decoration is necessary, it flies beautifully on days when the tree-tops are barely stirring in the wind. Any lightweight material is adequate but paper is not suitable. Scale patterns can be drawn on the material with felt pen or dye-paint; other decorations can be added with paper or scraps of fabric. If long flexible sticks are hard to find, make them by joining short flower-pot sticks together with wire.

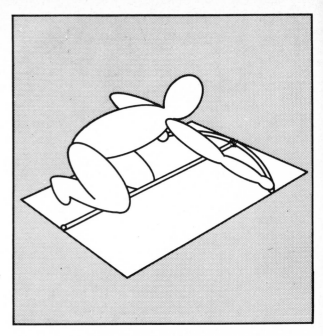

Stage 1 Lay the material flat. Cut the straight "backbone" stick to same length as material and lay it in the center of the material. With wire, firmly tie the center of the longest flexible stick to the top of the backbone stick. Then, kneeling on the backbone stick, bend the top stick downwards.

MATERIALS

1 straight, "backbone" stick about 54"/137 cm long

2 flexible sticks of even thickness 60"/152cm and 44"/112 cm long

1 large rectangle of lightweight fabric 56 x 42"/140 x 107 cm

Carpet tape

Colored fabric or paper for streamers

Scraps of fabric or paper for decoration

2 curtain rings

Garden or picture wire

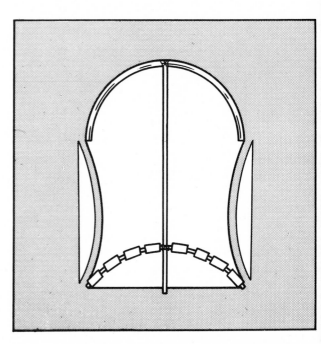

Stage 4 Keeping a gentle tension on the fabric in a downward direction, join the curved stick to the fabric with carpet tape. Remove the string. The floppy material on either side of the kite can now be trimmed away with scissors so that it has an even, waisted, fish-like shape.

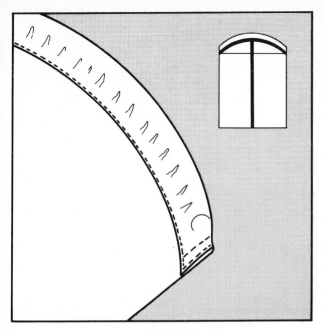

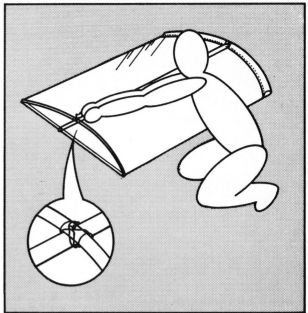

Stage 2 Join the ends of the top stick temporarily with string as if stringing a bow. Leaving a margin of about 1½" /4 cm trim the material around the curved stick, then turn the edges over and stitch them down so that the curved stick is enclosed in a strong hem; remove the string so that the material is stretched.

Stage 3 Bend the shorter flexible stick until its curve is approximately half that of the other and join the ends temporarily with string. Lay it on the bottom end of the kite so that its centerpoint rests on the backbone stick. Wire them together firmly.

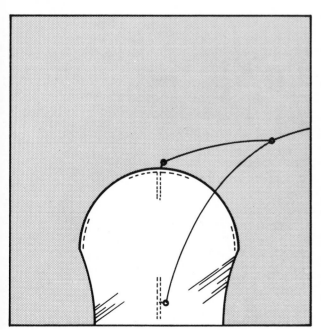

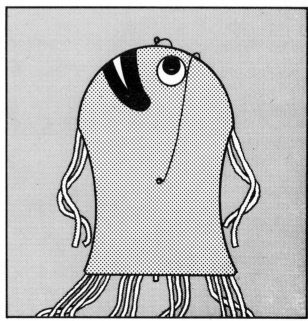

Stage 5 Below the mid-point of the backbone stick, cut a small hole in the fabric and wire a brass curtain ring to the stick. Also wire a ring to the top of the kite. Attach a two-part bridle (page 12) to the two rings. If the kite flies tail-heavy the lower ring may have to be moved down a little.

Stage 6 A beady eye and fat lips can be cut from paper or scraps of material and decorated with felt pens, then tacked to the kite with needle and thread. Streamers are made from strips of material or crêpe paper and stapled or stitched on. In strong winds add longer streamers.

Mother Turtle

A stately sea lady, Mother Turtle flies steadily ahead of her brood as if deaf to their laughter as they tumble and spiral joyfully behind her. The construction of the turtle, like the octopus, is a variation of the hexagonal design and shows that there is really no limit to the fascinating designs and shapes the imaginative kite-maker can achieve with a simple formula. The dark green material of the turtle's shell-back has been painted with ordinary paint normally used for decorating rooms. This paint has also been used on the paper plates that are the basis of the little turtles, some of which seem to be still coming out of their eggs.

MATERIALS

Large piece of colored material, about 52 x 46"/132 x 117 cm

4 straight sticks 44"/112 cm long

4 short lightweight sticks, two 12"/30 cm, two 7"/18 cm long

10 (or more) paper plates

Short piece of wire

2 long lengths of strong string

1 piece of stiff cardboard (cut from a packing box)

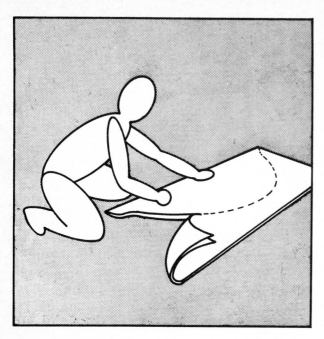

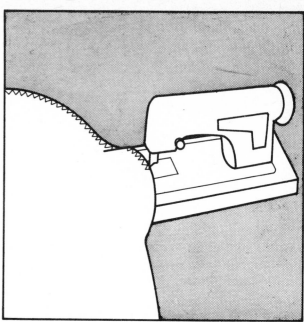

Stage 1 The outline of the kite is egg-shaped, sharper end uppermost. But the exact shape is unimportant as long as both sides are equal, so before cutting the material first fold it in half, then cut both sides together. Taper each end slightly for the neck and tail.

Stage 2 To prevent fraying either cut with pinking shears, machine-sew round using zig-zag stitch, or leave a margin of about ½″ /2 cm and turn up a narrow hem all the way round; (small V-cuts will be required at intervals to keep the curved outline).

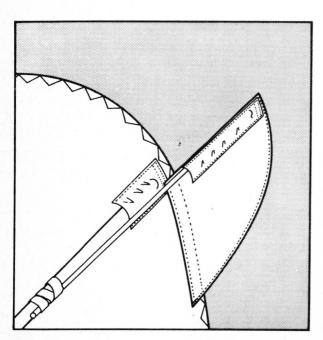

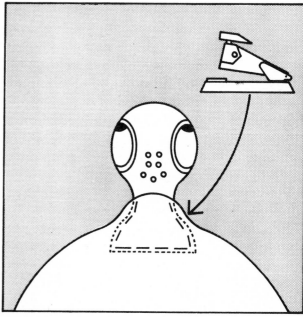

Stage 5 Cut four 6″/15 cm triangles (with one side slightly curved) of a different colored fabric, hem the edges to prevent fraying, and sew each one to the rim of the kite near the four diagonal pockets. To make the top ones jut out, make pockets for thin sticks and tape these sticks to the kite's main diagonal support sticks.

Stage 6 Cut a piece of stiff cardboard in the shape of the head and neck and paint large eyes. When dry, staple the neck to the top of the body. Patterns for the turtle's back can be painted, or made of patches of material and stuck on with fabric glue.

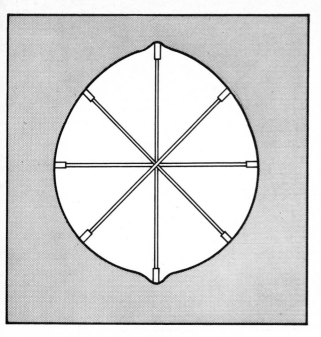

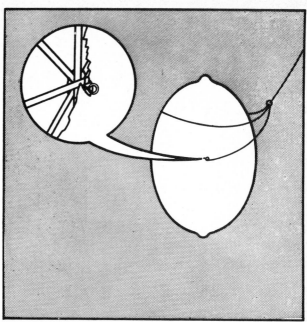

Stage 3 Spread the material face-down and cross two sticks on the vertical and horizontal center lines. Cross two more sticks over them as diagonals, cut the sticks to length, and sew on pockets into which the ends of the sticks will fit so the material is pulled gently taut (see page 28).

Stage 4 Make a single loop of wire over the meeting point of the sticks. Cut a small slit in the fabric below and tie a curtain ring to the wire. Attach a three-point bridle (see page 12) to the ring, and to the upper diagonal pockets as shown.

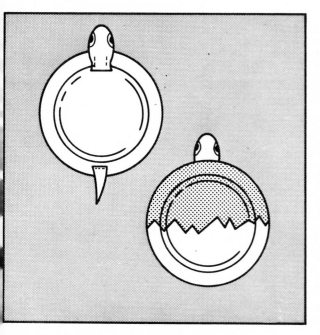

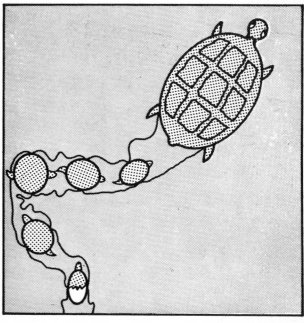

Stage 7 The baby turtles are made of paper plates; cut heads and tails from other paper plates and glue or staple them on. Then paint the stiff paper and add designs. It's fun if the last three or four babies look as if they're emerging from their eggs, as in the diagram.

Stage 8 Take two equal pieces of strong string or cord and safety-pin each to a back flipper. Then staple the baby turtles in a line between the two strings or cord.

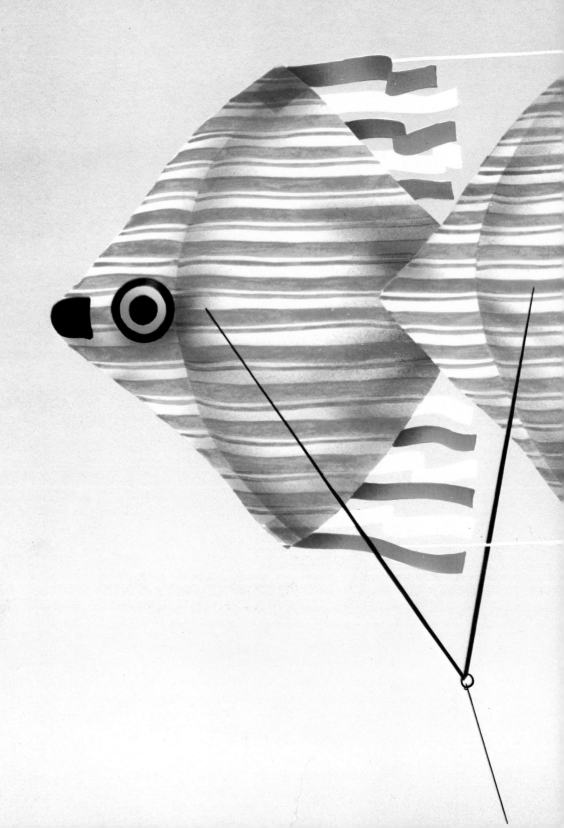

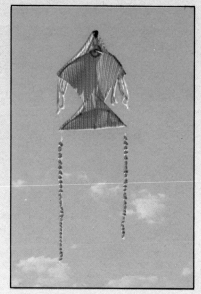

Angel~fish

Angel-fish

The fanciful pink-striped Angel-fish makes a pretty sight, trailing his streamers and long pink tail. It is a large, steady kite which in gusty conditions can sometimes lose the wind and dive: then you must give the line plenty of slack so that the weight of the tail brings the kite upright again and when it catches the wind in its fins it will soar up to cruise once more among the clouds. As the kite is made of fabric, it is easy to add additional decorations by stitching or stapling them on. The kite will bear a considerable weight of streamers and baubles which imaginative kite-makers can design from old wrapping paper, Christmas decorations, and scraps of bright material.

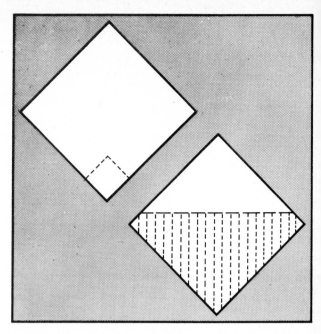

Stage 1 Take one square of material and cut a small square "bite" out of one corner. From the other square cut a large triangle and use the remaining material to cut up into streamers for adding to the tail and fins of the Angel-fish later.

MATERIALS

1 straight stick 60"/152 cm long
2 thin flexible sticks 56"/142 cm long
2 squares of striped material 36"/91 cm and 24"/61 cm
2 long pieces of string
4 curtain rings
Carpet tape
Short pieces of wire

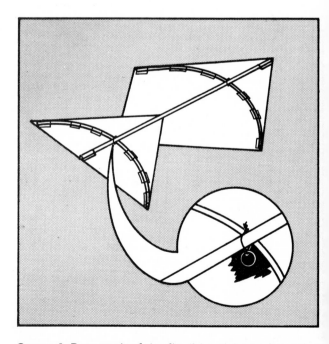

Stage 4 Bow each of the flexible sticks and slot the ends into opposite pockets, trimming the sticks to length as necessary. Fasten the fabric to the sticks with carpet tape. Wire each stick to the backbone stick; slit the fabric so a curtain ring can be attached to each wire and pulled to the front side.

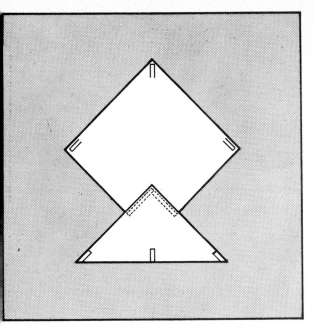

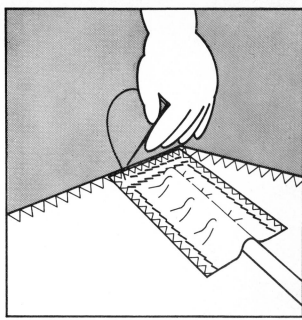

Stage 2 Sew the two pieces together as shown, using two strong seams. Hem or zig-zag stitch the edges all round, or trim with pinking shears, to prevent fraying. Choice of colors of the two sections is important; if they are striped, align the stripes exactly.

Stage 3 Sew thin pockets about 5"/12 cm long on each side, reinforcing the ends with double seams. Sew pockets 3"/8 cm long at the top and bottom of the kite. Cut the straight stick so that when the ends are inserted in the pockets the material is pulled gently taut.

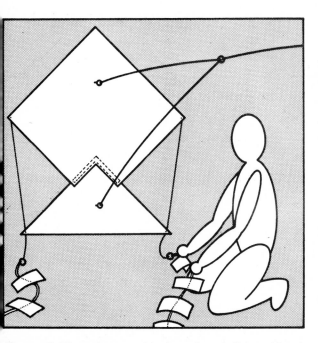

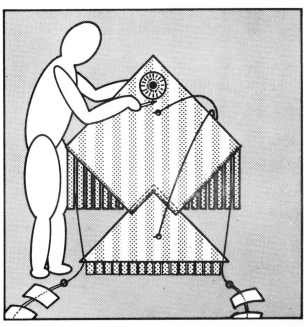

Stage 5 Tie strings to the tips of each fin and lead them back through holes in the tips of the fish's tail; tie curtain rings to the ends for attaching the tails (see page 11). To the two curtain rings on the front of the kite attach a two-part bridle (see page 12).

Stage 6 Each tail should be at least twice as long as the height of the kite. Streamers can be stitched or stapled to the trailing edges of the fish's fins, and to the bottom edge of his tail. His eye is made of a round piece of paper stitched on and decorated with felt pens.

KITES OF
MANY LANDS

Korean kite

Korean kite

The rectangular shape of this distinctive three-colored kite derives from what were probably the earliest kites flown in China. The idea spread to Korea well over a thousand years ago but while Chinese kites were developed in other shapes, the Korean kite, traditionally made of paper and bamboo, anything from 1'/30 cm to 4'/125 cm wide, stayed much the same. With tails this kite flies steadily and easily; without tails it is more exciting and you have to be quick to keep it in the air as it dives, somersaults, and slides sideways. Because it moves so quickly it was used by Korean peasants for kite-fighting games, as well as for serious ceremonial purposes such as offering symbolic sacrifices to heaven and the gods.

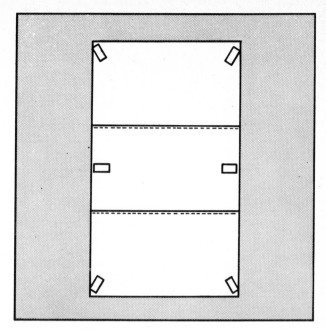

Stage 1 Cut the colored materials into three identical oblong shapes 34 x 20"/86 x 51 cm (or so that the width of the kite is three-fifths its height). Sew the pieces together with narrow, strong seams and protect the outside edges from fraying by turning a narrow hem or seaming.

MATERIALS

3 oblong pieces of colored lightweight material
34 x 20"/86 x 51 cm

3 straight sticks, two 64"/163 cm long, one
32"/81 cm long

1 curtain ring

1 patch of black fabric or crêpe paper about
12"/30 cm wide

2 long pieces of colored ribbon or crêpe paper

Stage 4 Mark the position of ring on the kite and temporarily remove the sticks. With the ring mark as the center point, use a short length of string and a marker pen as a drawing compass to inscribe a circle with a diameter about three-quarters of A — B. Cut out the circle with pinking shears.

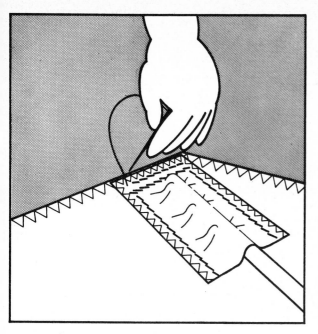

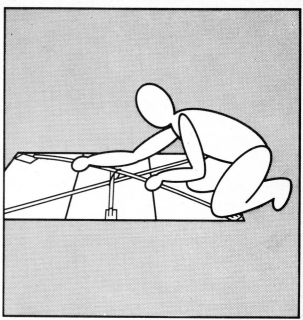

Stage 2 From spare scraps of material cut six pockets and sew them in the positions shown in Stage 1. Each pocket should be just wide enough to take the sticks and 2-3"/5-8 cm long. Reinforce the bottom of each pocket with a double seam for strength.

Stage 3 Cut the two horizontal sticks and the cross stick to lengths so that when they are inserted into the pockets, the kite is gently taut. Thread each of the sticks through a large curtain ring positioned where they cross. If necessary, the sticks will need to be curved upwards as they are inserted.

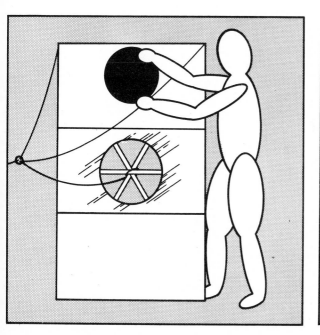

Stage 5 Replace sticks. Attach a three-part bridle (see page 12) to the upper corners of the kite and to the center ring. From black crêpe paper or fabric cut a round patch and sew it to the center of the top band of material using large stitches; this is part of the traditional design of the kite.

Stage 6 The kite flies more steadily if given a tail which can be made of long ribbons or strips of crêpe paper sewn, pinned or stapled to the bottom edge of the kite. If the kite rocks or dives excessively in the sky the tails should be lengthened or a third one added.

An unusual shape adapted from a traditional Chinese kite first flown centuries ago, the fan is interesting to fly: as the wind gets stronger its wings bend further and further back so it is always steady in flight. It needs a long tail for stability but this doesn't hold it down. The black material stands out against a bright sky. The Chinese character which reads "good luck" is written in vivid orange ribbon tacked to the material with needle and thread. The kite can also be made with material of more delicate colors on which traditional Chinese designs can be painted.

Chinese Fan

MATERIALS

5 straight sticks, four about 38"/96 cm long, one about 40"/102 cm long

1 flexible stick 66"/168 cm long

1 piece of material about 54"/137 cm square

Carpet tape

Short pieces of wire

2 curtain rings

Brightly colored ribbon

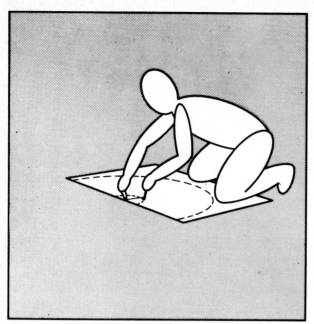

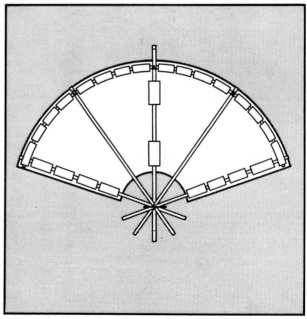

Stage 1 Lay the material flat. Using a length of string and marker pen as a drawing compass, inscribe a semi-circle (radius about 34"/86 cm) which will be the outer edge of the kite. From the same center point inscribe a small circle (radius about 4"/102 mm) which will be the lower perimeter of the kite. Cut along the marked lines.

Stage 2 Cut four sticks 3"/8 cm longer than the radius of the outer edge of the fan and one stick 4"/10 cm longer. Drill a small hole at the tip of each stick. The longer stick needs two holes about 1"/3 cm apart. Lay these on the material as shown, evenly spaced round the fan. Mark where they cross, and drill a hole in each. The long stick requires a second hole near the bottom.

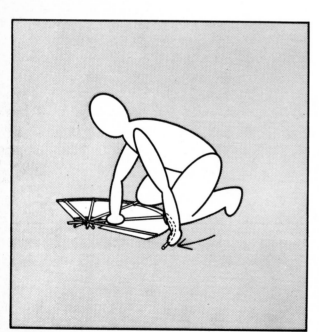

Stage 5 Wire the center of the flexible stick to the lower of the two holes in the top of the stick A so the flexible stick is underneath A. Then bend the top stick into a curve and wire it to the top of each of the other sticks making use of the drilled holes.

Stage 6 Using short strips of carpet tape, firmly fix the frame to the fabric. The tape needs to be stuck only to the top curved stick, the outermost sticks, and in one or two places to the center stick. Ensure that a good strong bond is obtained.

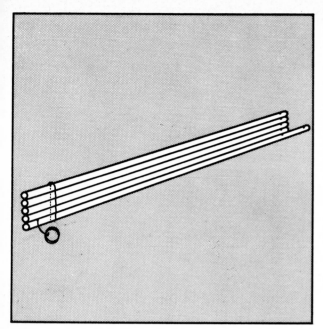

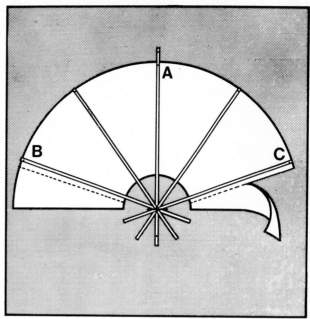

Stage 3 Lay the sticks one on top of the other, the longer center stick at the bottom, so their lower holes are aligned. Thread wire through the holes, loop it round the sticks, and join it underneath. Tie on a curtain ring to the bottom stick for attaching the tail and bridle later.

Stage 4 Fan the sticks out and place them on the material. The longer center stick A must be vertical; the outermost ones B and C should lie at an angle of about 80° to it with the intermediate sticks halfway between them. Leaving a 1"/3 cm margin, trim the material from either side.

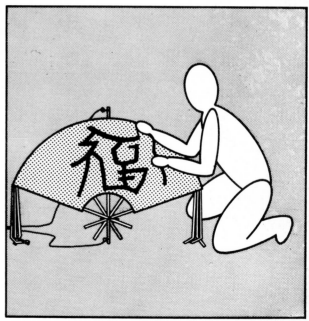

Stage 7 To the hole at the top of the center stick wire the remaining curtain ring or make a small loop of wire. Attach a two-part bridle (see page 12) to this and the ring at the bottom of the center stick. The kite can now be test-flown.

Stage 8 Write the Chinese character meaning 'good luck' on the kite, using narrow ribbon sewn on with long tacking stitches, or paint on the pattern with dye paints. Short lengths of ribbon of the same color look good if made into tassles sewn or stapled to each side of the fan.

Nagasaki
Fighting kite

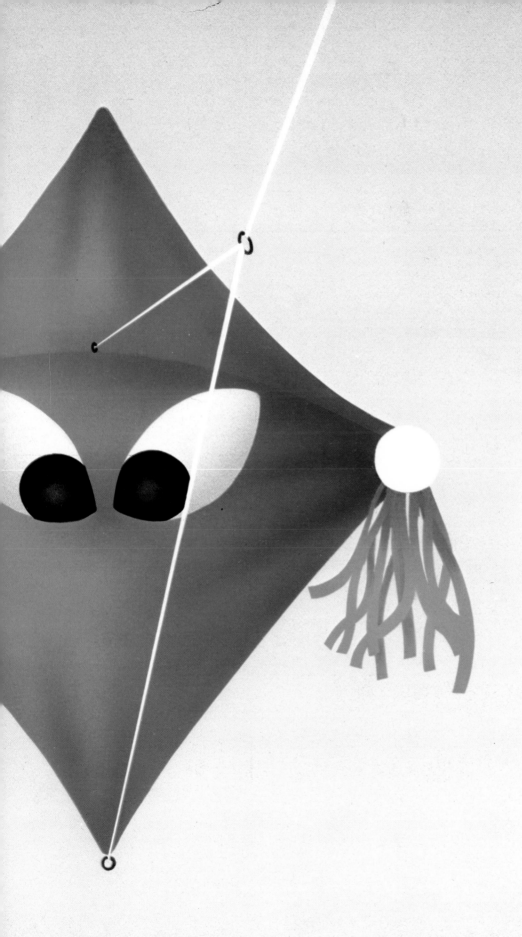

Nagasaki Fighting kite

The striking feature of this fierce-looking Japanese fighting kite is its simplicity — a square of lightweight material and two sticks are all that is required. In kite-fighting contests, Japanese villagers sharpened their kite strings with glue and ground glass, then tried to cut each other down. The kite flies strongly without a tail as long as it's perfectly symmetrical and well balanced. The eyes are not a traditional part of the design but seem appropriate for a kite made to hunt down and cut loose other kites. It certainly gives small dogs at ground level something to bark at!

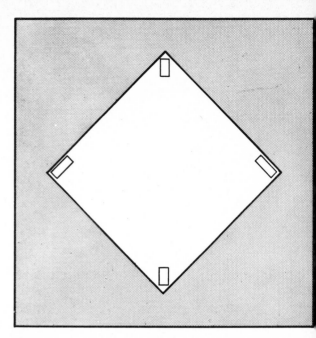

Stage 1 Choose a lightweight, brightly colored material and check that it is square. Hem, zig-zag stitch or trim with pinking shears any edges that are liable to fray in the wind. Mark the positions of the pockets and cut them from waste material.

MATERIALS

1 square of light material about 36"/91 cm square and some small scraps
1 straight stick 50"/127 cm long
1 flexible stick 53"/135 cm long
2 curtain rings
Small piece of polyethylene
Scraps of black crêpe paper
Colored tissue paper

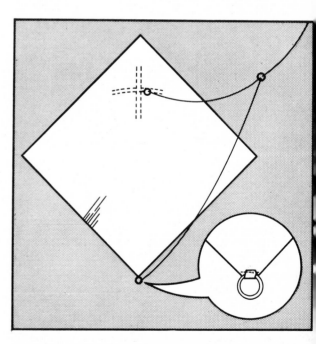

Stage 4 Sew a curtain ring to the bottom of the kite and attach a two-part bridle (see page 12). It is important that each side of the kite is exactly symmetrical; if one side is heavier, shave a little wood off the cross-stick. The kite can now be test-flown.

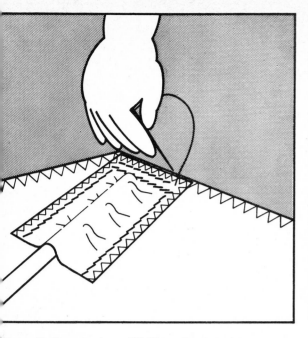

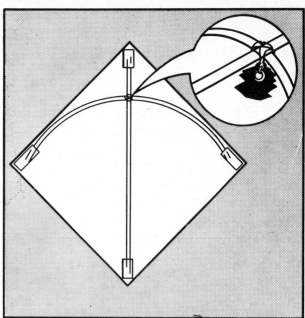

Stage 2 Sew pockets 3″/7 cm long at the top and bottom corners and cut the straight stick so that when the ends are inserted the kite is pulled gently taut. In the other corners sew pockets about 5″/12 cm long. Reinforce the ends of the pockets with double seams for strength.

Stage 3 Bow the flexible stick and insert the ends in the pockets. The point where the flexible stick crosses the other should be about one quarter of the distance down the kite; wire them together. Slit the fabric beneath the joint and make a small loop of wire or attach a curtain ring.

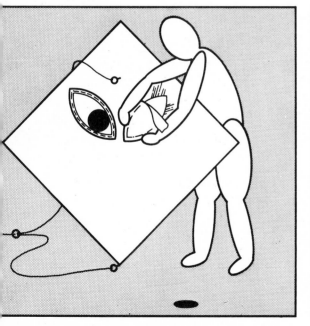

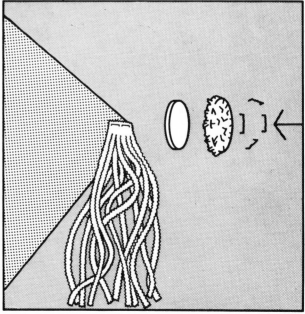

Stage 5 To make transparent eyes first cut a template of cardboard to the required shape, then lay it on the kite and cut around it. Cut pieces of polythylene 1″/3 cm larger all round, place them over the holes, then sew them on with large stitches.

Stage 6 The eyeballs are made of black crêpe paper which are cut out and sewn on the polyethylene in the same way. Tassles for each side are made of thin strips of tissue paper stapled to discs of cardboard which are covered in silver paper and stapled or sewn to the kite.

Malayan Bow

Malayan Bow

The age-old bowed kites from Malaya and Indonesia are high-flying steady kites that do not need tails. It was because of their steadiness that late last century they were adapted by Western scientists for use in some of the first advanced meteorological experiments. The first Malay kites were made of sewn leaves and contests were held in paddy fields for the highest kite, the most beautiful kite, and battles were fought in which fliers tried to use their own kites to saw through the strings of others. This particular kite retains the traditional shape but has been adapted for modern materials and easy construction; it is also bowed in two directions fore and aft as well as from side to side.

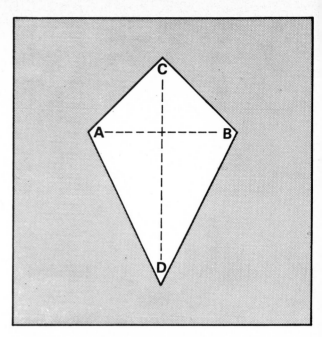

Stage 1 Cut the material to a symmetrical diamond shape so that the line AB crosses the line CD about one-third of the distance from the top of the kite. Use pinking shears, seam a hem or sew all round with zig-zag stitch to prevent fraying.

MATERIALS

2 straight sticks 56"/142 cm and 40"/102 cm long

1 piece of brightly colored material oblong in shape about 56 x 40"/142 x 102 cm

1 piece of broad ribbon about 12'/4 m long, 1¼"/4 cm wide

2 short pieces of wire

2 curtain rings

Colored paper and cardboard for decoration

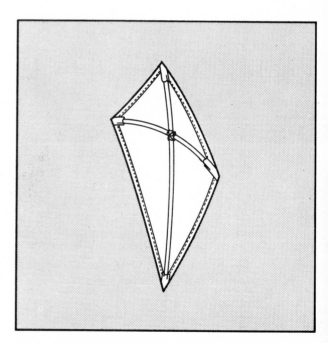

Stage 4 Rotate the sticks so that they bow firmly against the fabric of the kite and make it taut. Ensure that the sticks cross at right angles and bind them together with wire. Slit the fabric below the joint and attach a curtain ring to the wire.

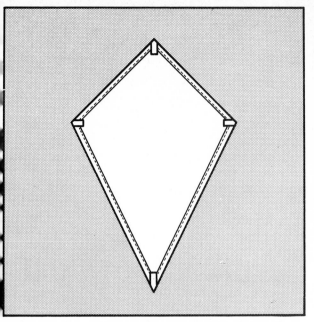

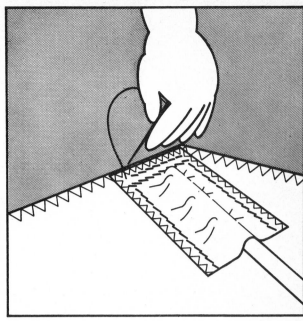

Stage 2 Fraying can also be prevented by sewing a broad ribbon all the way round. This shows up nicely with the light behind it and if its color contrasts with that of the kite looks very pretty indeed. Finish off the corners tidily.

Stage 3 In each corner sew a pocket 2-3"/5-8 cm long and just wide enough to take the sticks as shown in Stage 2. Reinforce the ends of the pockets with double seams for strength. Cut the sticks about 1"/3 cm longer than necessary so that they must be curved as they are inserted into the pockets.

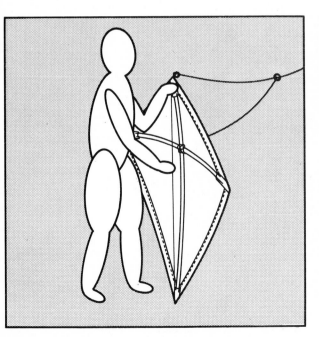

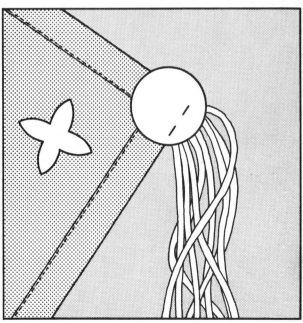

Stage 5 Sew the second brass curtain ring to the top of the kite. Attach a two-part bridle (see page 12) to the rings. The kite can now be test-flown. If the sticks do not bow easily, a piece of string can be fixed from C to D (as if stringing a bow) and adjusted as needed.

Stage 6 Round pieces of cardboard covered with tinfoil, and stars cut from colored Christmas wrapping paper, can be stapled or sewn to the kite for effective and traditional decoration. Make the tassles from thin strips of crêpe paper and staple them to the cardboard.

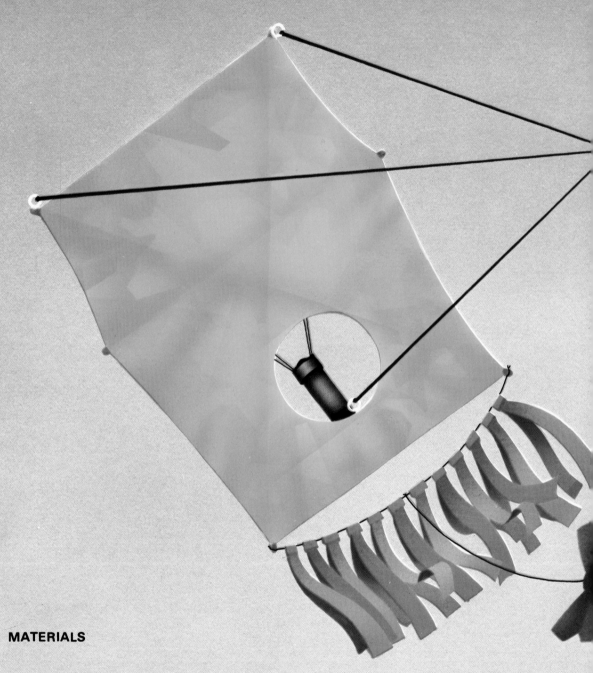

MATERIALS

2 sheets of gold wrapping paper or similar
material
3 straight sticks, two 35"/89 cm and one
26"/66 cm long
2 short sticks 12"/30 cm and 8""/20 cm long
Garden or picture wire
String
Cellophane tape
3 curtain rings

82

Golden Dragon

Breathing fire and brimstone, the golden dragon kite should perhaps be called the Yellow Peril. The dense orange smoke streaming from his mouth makes a magnificent sight against a bright blue sky. In fact it comes from a yachtsman's daylight distress flare which has been tied to the kite's frame. For obvious reasons the dragon should not breathe his smoke anywhere near the coast! The kite is a traditional Chinese design which can be anything from 2'/60 cm to 6'/2 m high. To complete the traditional picture, it ought to have a string of loud fire-crackers attached to its tail. Made of shiny gold Christmas wrapping paper on a simple frame, it is quick and easy to make and requires no sewing.

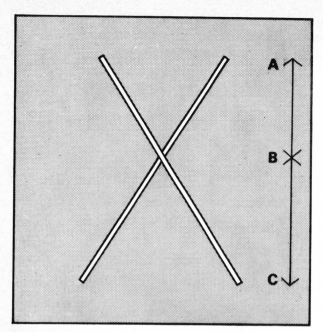

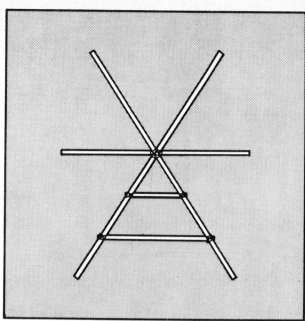

Stage 1 Lay the two longest sticks so they form a tall narrow X and cross at a point less than halfway down their lengths, as shown. In other words, the distance between A and B is a little less than the distance between B and C.

Stage 2 Lay the third stick horizontally across them as shown and wire the sticks together tightly. To the bottom part of the cross, wire two short sticks equidistant from center and bottom of the kite.

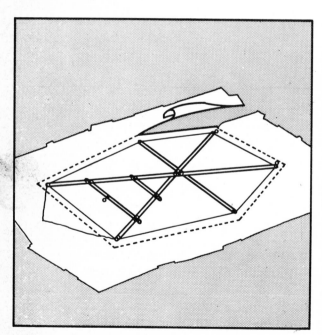

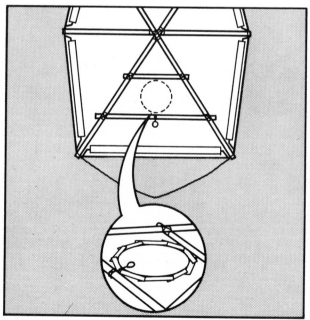

Stage 5 Join together with clear cellophane tape sheets of shiny Christmas wrapping paper or any other kind of light but strong decorative material (polyethylene will also serve). Lay the frame on the paper and cut around it leaving a margin of 1"/3 cm.

Stage 6 Fold the edges of the paper over the frame and stick down firmly with cellophane tape. Between the two horizontal sticks in the lower part of the frame cut a neat round hole as the dragon's mouth; reinforce the edges with cellophane tape so that the paper won't tear in the wind.

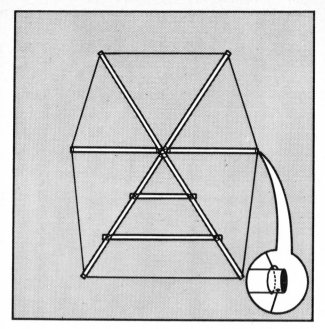

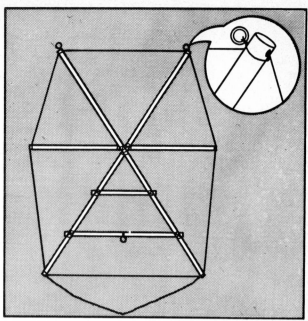

Stage 3 Drill a thin hole in the ends of each stick and with thin garden wire or picture wire or strong twine join each to the paper. This "web" must be taut and strong, but not so taut that the sticks of the frame are bent or distorted: an even tension all round is needed.

Stage 4 Wire a curtain ring to each of the top points of the kite and wire the third ring to the center of the lower cross-piece. Attach a three-part bridle (see page 12) to these rings after the kite has been covered. Attach a slack loop of wire between the two bottom points.

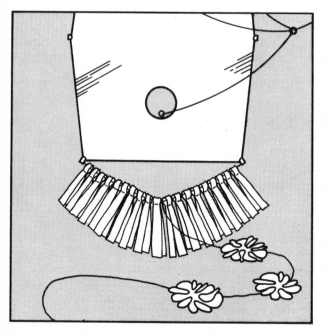

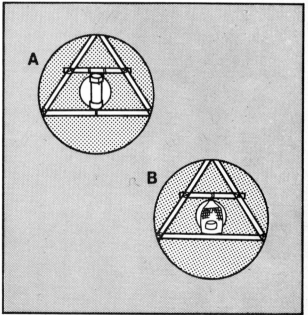

Stage 7 The dragon's beard is made by stapling tassles of paper over the loop of wire below the kite. The dragon's tail (see page 10), made of rosettes of colored paper joined by string or tape, is attached to the center of this loop. Many other spirals and tassles of paper can be added.

Stage 8 You should make your dragon breathe smoke only when adults are present and when the conditions are quite safe.Smoke candle A of the type sold in sporting goods stores is ideal because it is safe and foolproof. Smoke pellets B, enclosed in a small wire-gauze bag, can also be used.

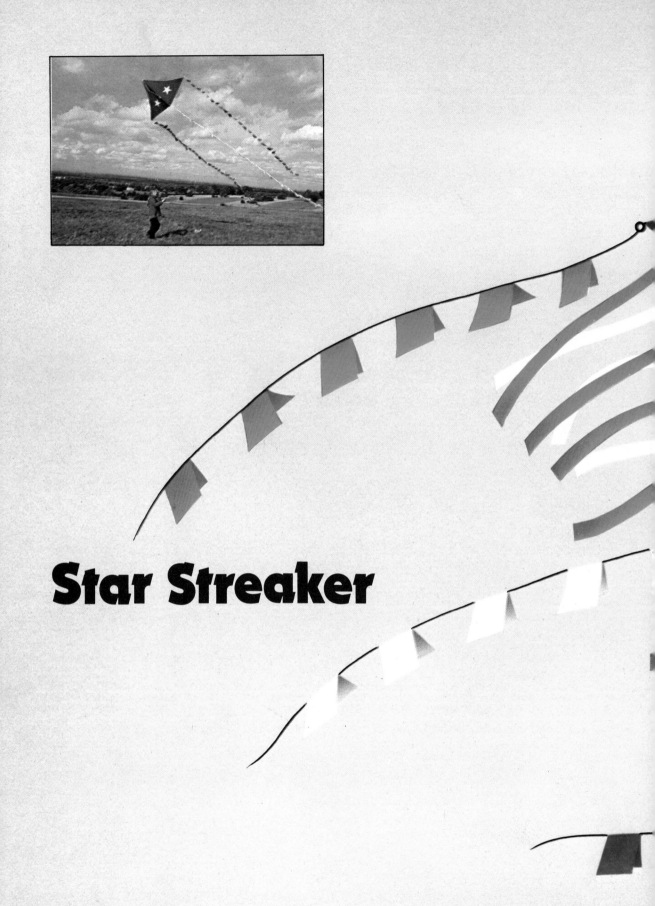

Star Streaker

Star Streaker

Spangled with glory like a homewards-zooming command module from space, the Star Streaker kite flies vigorously, trailing its multi-colored tails like jet-streams. The delta profile looks exciting in the sky and is great fun to fly. Apart from its stars and stripes decoration, this kite is genuinely American in concept because it was adapted from the magnificently complicated multi-celled tetrahedral kites flown by this country's great scientific pioneer and inventor of the telephone, Alexander Graham Bell. At the turn of the century he flew kites as part of his researches into flight. One kite, known as the Cygnet, had 3,393 cells, was towed by a ferry-boat, and lifted a U.S. Army lieutenant to 168 feet. The kite pictured here collapses for convenient carrying and can be 2-8'/60 cm - 245 cm wide.

Stage 1 To ensure that the kite is symmetrical in shape first double the material over so that both sides of the kite are cut simultaneously. The nose of the kite should be approximately a right angle. Zig-zag stitch or hem the raw edges to prevent fraying.

MATERIALS

1 large piece of fabric about 72"/183 cm square
4 strong straight sticks, one 62"/157 cm and three 39"/99 cm long
4 curtain rings
Small piece of cardboard
Scraps of fabric

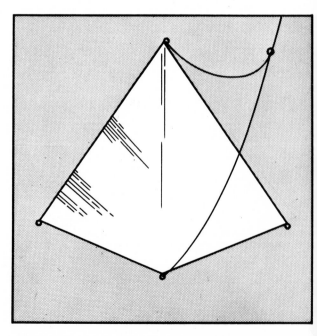

Stage 4 Sew a curtain ring to each of the four points of the kite. The three along the trailing edge are for attaching the tails (see page 11) which are made of square patches of colored fabric. The center one is also used for attaching a two-part bridle (see page 12)

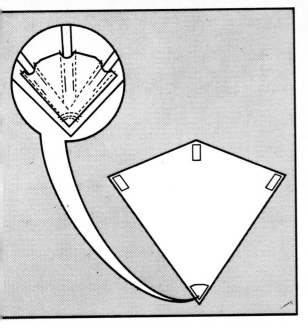

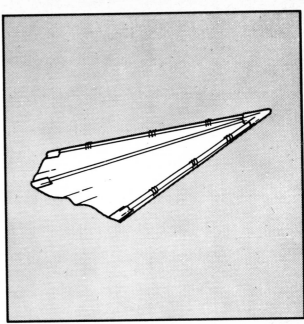

Stage 2 From scraps of material cut four pockets for the positions shown above. The large pocket in the nose must take three sticks. Reinforce the ends with double seams for strength. Bend the sticks to insert them in the pockets: the fabric should be gently taut.

Stage 3 Sew the sticks down to the edges of the kite as shown. If bamboo sticks are used the thick ends should be at the back of the kite.

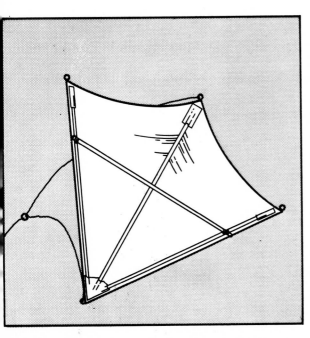

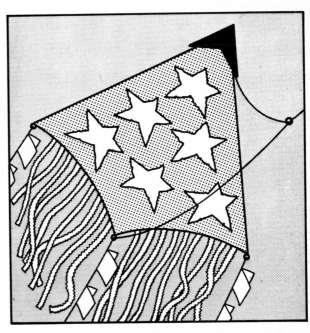

Stage 5 Attach a horizontal stick between the two outside sticks to keep the kite rigid. Bind it on firmly with string or wire so it can be adjusted backwards or forwards for strong winds (wings steeply angled) or light breezes (kite nearly flat).

Stage 6 A red cardboard arrowhead stapled to the nose makes the kite look more exciting. The fabric can be decorated with silver stars made of tinfoil or Christmas paper. Red and white streamers made of paper or fabric can be stapled to the trailing edge between the tails.

INVENTORY 1983